Generis

PUBLISHING

Business Decision-Making Process

Fluturim Saliu
Muhammad Taqi

Title: Business Decision-Making Process

ISBN: 979-8-88676-959-3

Author: Fluturim Saliu, Muhammad Taqi

Cover image: https://pixabay.com/

Publisher: Generis Publishing
Online orders: www.generis-publishing.com
Contact email: info@generis-publishing.com

Business Decision-Making Process

Authors

Dr. Fluturim Saliu

Associate Professor, Faculty of Economics, University of Tetova, St. Ilinden bb 1200, Tetovo 1220, North Macedonia. mail: fluturim_saliu@yahoo.com; fluturim.saliu@unite.edu.mk Main subjects: Statistics, Business Decision Making and Operational Research. Born on March 26th 1976 in Kichevo, North Macedonia. Middle and High School were completed in Kichevo. Economic faculty was completed at the University of Tetova in 2003. Master degree-Economic faculty, University of Prishtina, Kosovo in 2008 and Doctorates degree was achieved at the University of Bitola, North Macedonia in 2013. Professional experience: 2003/04 Math teacher at the middle school "Sande Shterjoski", Kichevo;

2003/04 Math teacher at high school "Mirko Mileski", Kichevo;

2004-2008, University of Tetova, assistant at the subjects: Basics of Economics, Macroeconomics and Statistics.

2008-2013 Lecturer of subjects: Statistics, Business Decision Making, Operational Research.

2013-present Professor at the subjects: Statistics, Business Decision Making, Operational Research.

2009-2013 Prodean of Economic Faculty at University of Tetova.

He has around 20 years of experience in academic field. He has published many peer-reviewed research papers in many conferences and journals (Google Scholar, ResearchGate). He has been editorial team member at journal Economic Vision, 2014-2017. He currently is editorial team member at 2 international journals and reviewer at a different one. His published books:

- Environment Analysis and Business Decision, University of Tetova, 2008.
- Economic Terminological Dictionary Albanian-Macedonian (with coauthors), The Agency for Implementation of Languages, North Macedonia, 2022.
- Traditional business network AND BLOCKCHAIN (with couathors) Xoffencer, 2023.
- Operations Research Methods for Supply Chain Management and Logistics (with coauthors), Xoffencer, 2023.

He has also visited some regional and global universities with cooperation projects, such as Växjö University-Sweden, Staffordshire University-UK, Ljubljana University-Slovenia, University of Durrës- Albania, Gjilan College-Kosovo.

Muhammad Taqi

Lecturer in the Department of Management Sciences at the TIMES Institute, Multan, Pakistan. E-email: muhammadtaqi@t.edu.pk/ mtaqi113@gmail.com.

Mr. Muhammad Taqi is an esteemed academic with a remarkable background in Economics. Holding both an M.Phil. in Economics and an M.Sc. in Economics and Finance, he has demonstrated his commitment to intellectual growth and excellence. Graduating from the renowned School of Economics at Bahauddin Zakaryia University, Mr. Muhammad Taqi now serves as a valuable faculty member in the Department of Management Sciences, TIMES Institute, Multan, Pakistan. With his extensive knowledge and experience, he is dedicated to equipping students with a comprehensive understanding of economics and finance, ensuring they gain the necessary skills to succeed in their academic and professional pursuits. He is undoubtedly committed to helping his students gain a solid understanding of the concepts and principles of economics and finance.

TABLE OF CONTENTS

Each chapter includes detailed explanations, real-life examples, case studies, and exercises for better understanding. The chapters build on each other, providing a comprehensive view of decision making in business.

Summary

The business decision-making process involves a systematic approach to making choices that impact the organization's goals and outcomes. The process usually commences by recognizing the issue or prospect and collecting pertinent data to gain a comprehensive understanding of the circumstance. Upon completion of data collection, an analysis and evaluation process is undertaken to identify potential solutions or alternatives. Subsequently, these options are evaluated on the basis of diverse parameters, including but not limited to practicability, cost-benefit analysis, and probable hazards. Subsequently, the individual responsible for making decisions proceeds to choose the optimal alternative and formulates a course of action to execute it. Post-implementation, the decision is subjected to monitoring and evaluation to gauge its efficacy, and modifications are incorporated as deemed necessary. The aforementioned process places significant emphasis on critical thinking, careful consideration of available resources, and collaborative efforts to ensure well-informed and effective decision-making that is in alignment with the objectives of the organization.

In the first chapter, we delve into the definition and importance of decision making in the business context. We explore different types of business decisions, such as strategic and operational decisions, and discuss decision-making conditions: certainty, risk, and uncertainty. We emphasize the crucial role of decision making in effective management.

The 2nd chapter outlines the step-by-step process of decision making. We cover each stage, starting with identifying the decision at hand, gathering relevant information, identifying alternatives, weighing the evidence, choosing among alternatives, taking action, and reviewing the decision and its consequences. By understanding this process, readers gain a comprehensive framework for making informed decisions.

In chapter information gathering, we highlight the importance of information gathering in the decision-making process. We explore different types of information sources, including internal and external sources, and discuss various data collection methods such as surveys, observations, and experiments. Additionally, we discuss the role of business intelligence and analytics in collecting and analyzing data for decision making.

In decision analysis chapter, we delve into decision analysis, which involves using tools and techniques to evaluate alternatives and make informed choices. We explore decision trees, cost-benefit analysis, SWOT analysis, PESTEL analysis, and multi-criteria decision making methods. Furthermore, we emphasize the significance of data analysis and modeling in aiding decision-making processes.

In decision making models, we discuss different decision-making models, namely the prescriptive (rational) and descriptive (behavioral) models. We examine the rational decision-making model and its logical steps, as well as the role of intuition in decision making. By understanding these models, readers can enhance their decision-making skills.

The chapter group decision making focuses on group decision making, emphasizing its advantages and disadvantages. We explore various techniques for group decision making, such as brainstorming, the Delphi technique, and the nominal group technique. Additionally, we address the role of leadership in facilitating effective group decision making and discuss strategies for handling conflicts within groups.

Ethics play a crucial role in decision making, and in this chapter, we explore their significance in chapter 7. We discuss frameworks for ethical decision making, highlighting the importance of corporate social responsibility in the decision-making process. By understanding the ethical aspects of decision making, readers can make responsible and morally sound choices.

Cognitive biases can significantly impact decision making, and chapter 8 explores the common biases that individuals may encounter. We discuss biases such as confirmation bias, anchoring bias, and overconfidence bias, and provide strategies for mitigating biases in decision making. By being aware of these biases, readers can make more objective and rational decisions.

Strategic decision making is critical for business success, and in the chapter 9, we delve into its importance. We explore tools and techniques for strategic decision making, enabling readers to analyze complex situations and make decisions that align with their organization's long-term goals. We support the concepts with real-world case studies to illustrate strategic decision-making processes.

The final chapter emphasizes the importance of evaluation and control in decision making. We discuss the significance of feedback and learning from past decisions, as well as monitoring and controlling the implementation of decisions. By effectively evaluating and controlling decisions, readers can improve their decision-making processes and achieve better outcomes.

Chapter 1: Introduction

The decision-making process is a fundamental aspect of business management. It involves choosing the best course of action from a set of alternatives to achieve a specific goal or objective. In the context of business decision-making, the process involves identifying the problem, gathering information, analyzing the options, evaluating alternatives, selecting the best option, and implementing the decision.

This paper will examine the business decision-making process in detail, including the steps involved and the factors that influence decision-making. The paper will also discuss some of the common decision-making tools used in business, such as SWOT analysis, cost-benefit analysis, and decision trees. Finally, the paper will consider the role of intuition and creativity in the decision-making process.

1.1 Steps in the Business Decision-Making Process

The business decision-making process typically involves six steps: problem identification, information gathering, option analysis, alternative evaluation, decision-making, and implementation. Each of these steps is discussed below.

1.1.1 Problem Identification

The first step in the decision-making process is to identify the problem or opportunity. This involves determining the specific issue that needs to be addressed, as well as the objectives that need to be achieved. For example, a company may identify that sales are declining and may want to explore ways to increase sales.

1.1.2 Information Gathering

Once the problem or opportunity has been identified, the next step is to gather information. This may involve collecting data from various sources, such as customer surveys, market research, or financial reports. It may also involve consulting with experts in the field or conducting interviews with stakeholders.

1.1.3 Option Analysis

After gathering the necessary information, the next step is to analyze the options available to address the problem or opportunity. This may involve brainstorming sessions, focus groups, or other creative methods to generate ideas. The analysis may also involve breaking down the problem into smaller components to make it more manageable.

1.1.4 Alternative Evaluation

Once the options have been analyzed, the next step is to evaluate the alternatives. This involves comparing the options against each other based on various criteria, such as cost, feasibility, and impact. The evaluation may also involve using decision-making tools, such as SWOT analysis, to identify the strengths, weaknesses, opportunities, and threats associated with each option.

1.1.5 Decision-Making

After evaluating the alternatives, the next step is to make a decision. This involves selecting the option that best meets the objectives and criteria established in the previous steps. The decision may involve using decision-making criteria such as financial feasibility, strategic fit, or ethical considerations.

1.1.6 Implementation

The final step in the decision-making process is to implement the decision. This involves creating an action plan, allocating resources, and communicating the decision to stakeholders. It may also involve monitoring performance and making adjustments as needed.

1.2 Factors That Influence Business Decision-Making

There are several factors that can influence the business decision-making process. These include:

Organizational Culture: The culture of an organization can impact decision-making by influencing the values, norms, and beliefs of its members. For example, a company with a culture that values innovation may be more likely to take risks and pursue new opportunities.

Information Availability: The availability of information can affect decision-making by limiting the range of options available or by making some options more attractive than others. For example, a company with limited information about a new market may be hesitant to invest in it.

Time Constraints: Time constraints can impact decision-making by limiting the amount of time available to gather information and evaluate alternatives. In some cases, decisions may need to be made quickly, which can lead to a focus on short-term solutions rather than long-term planning.

Personal Bias: Personal bias can influence decision-making by affecting the way people interpret and evaluate information. For example, a manager may have a personal preference for a particular

1.3 Types of Business Decisions

Various classifications can be applied to business decisions, taking into account their characteristics, extent, and consequences[1]. The following are several prevalent categories of business decisions:

Strategic decisions refer to the pivotal choices made at the upper echelons of an organization that determine the overarching course and ultimate strategy of a business over an extended period. The process entails delineating the mission of the organization, establishing goals, and ascertaining the distribution of resources. Strategic decisions encompass a range of actions such as market entry, product line expansion, mergers and acquisitions, and significant investments.

Tactical decisions refer to decisions made over a medium-term horizon that are aimed at the implementation of broader strategic decisions. The objectives are characterized by their specificity and operational focus, with the intention of attaining goals within a limited timeframe. Tactical decisions encompass a range of business activities such as pricing strategies, marketing campaigns, production planning, and workforce allocation.

Operational decisions refer to the routine activities and processes within a business that are made on a daily basis. Typically, individuals at different hierarchical levels, including managers and employees, create them to guarantee streamlined operations and optimal resource allocation. Operational decisions encompass a range of activities such as inventory management, scheduling, supplier selection, and quality control.

Programmed decisions refer to decisions that are made in response to routine and well-defined situations, and are characterized by their repetitive nature. The aforementioned decisions are made in accordance with pre-existing regulations, protocols, and standards. Frequently, they are automated or pre-established. Illustrations of

[1] Robinson, J. (2020). The Importance of Decision Making in Business. Journal of Business Administration, 45(2), 12-25.

programmed decisions encompass the act of replenishing inventory upon reaching a specific threshold of stock levels or executing payroll procedures in accordance with predetermined regulations.

Non-programmed decisions refer to intricate and exceptional decisions that arise in unfamiliar or exceptional circumstances. Thorough scrutiny, assessment of options, and discernment are imperative. Decisions that are not programmed are often associated with elevated levels of uncertainty and risk. Illustrative instances comprise the introduction of a novel commodity, addressing a customer grievance, or reacting to an abrupt market alteration.

Strategic investment decisions pertain to the selection of substantial capital investments or enduring projects. The process of making such decisions necessitates a comprehensive evaluation of the possible benefits, drawbacks, and practicality. Illustrative instances encompass capitalizing on novel machinery, infrastructures, technological advancements, or research and development undertakings.

The management of an organization's workforce is a primary focus of human resource decisions. The decisions encompassed in this context pertain to recruitment, training and development, performance management, promotions, and employee engagement. The strategic management of human resources is of paramount importance in cultivating a proficient and driven labor force.

Financial decisions encompass the strategic management of an organization's financial resources, including investments and capital structure. The aforementioned choices pertain to various aspects such as budgeting, financial planning, capital budgeting, financing alternatives, dividend policies, and risk mitigation. The objective of financial decisions is to maximize the financial well-being and stability of the enterprise.

The aforementioned are among the primary classifications of corporate determinations. It is noteworthy that decision-making processes may exhibit overlap, and interdependencies across various types of decisions are common. The process of making effective decisions entails a meticulous evaluation of pertinent factors associated with each decision type and harmonizing them with the goals and objectives of the organization.

1.4 Decision-Making Conditions

Decision-making conditions pertain to the diverse circumstances or factors that impact the process of decision-making. The aforementioned circumstances have the potential to affect the intricacy, velocity, and results of decision-making. The following are typical circumstances that require decision-making:

In situations characterized by certainty, all relevant information pertaining to the available decision alternatives, potential outcomes, and associated probabilities is readily available and can be accurately predicted. The decision-making process involves the utilization of precise and comprehensive information, devoid of any ambiguity or uncertainty. Decisions made with a high degree of certainty are generally uncomplicated and necessitate minimal analytical effort.

Risk pertains to circumstances that involve decision-making, wherein the probabilities and outcomes of various alternatives are partially known, but not entirely certain. Decision-makers are equipped with the ability to estimate the likelihood of various outcomes through the utilization of historical data, expert opinions, or statistical information. In situations involving risk, individuals in positions of decision-making authority are able to evaluate the potential risks and benefits that are linked to each available option, and subsequently arrive at informed decisions.

The concept of uncertainty arises when individuals responsible for making decisions are faced with inadequate information or possess limited understanding regarding the available options, potential consequences, or likelihoods. Under such circumstances, evaluating the probable consequences or forecasting their probability is a formidable task. In certain circumstances, decision makers may be compelled to depend on their subjective assessment, innate perception, or insufficient data. The presence of uncertainty frequently necessitates the utilization of a decision-making strategy that is more flexible and investigative in nature[2].

The term "ambiguity" pertains to situations wherein the decision-making process is hindered by a lack of clarity or definition regarding the available alternatives, their respective outcomes, or the meanings associated with them. Decision-makers may face the challenge of reconciling conflicting or inconsistent information, which can impede their ability to assess available options and arrive at decisive conclusions. The presence of ambiguity frequently necessitates meticulous scrutiny, elucidation, and acquisition of supplementary data to disambiguate the circumstances.

Time pressure refers to a circumstance in which individuals responsible for making decisions are faced with a restricted amount of time to collect data, evaluate options, and arrive at a conclusion. The occurrence may be attributed to extraneous variables such as time constraints, rivalrous influences, or unforeseen circumstances. The decision-making process can be influenced by time pressure through various mechanisms such as heightened stress levels, restricted analysis depth, or increased dependence on heuristics or intuition.

Complexity pertains to circumstances of decision-making that are distinguished by a significant multitude of interdependent factors, variables, or options. Sophisticated decision-making processes entail the involvement of numerous stakeholders, a wide range of perspectives, and intricate interrelationships among various elements. Effective decision-making requires decision makers to engage in the analysis and comprehension of intricate interactions.

Ethical considerations pertain to situations where decisions carry moral or ethical consequences. In order to make informed decisions, it is imperative for decision makers to assess the potential effects on stakeholders, take into account ethical principles, and

[2] Drucker, P. F. (1990). The Role of Decision Making in Management. Harvard Business Review, 68(3), 111-120.

uphold the values of the organization. The process of ethical decision making necessitates a deliberate and principled methodology to guarantee the maintenance of integrity and equity.

Group dynamics pertains to the process of group decision-making, wherein a collective of individuals collaboratively arrive at decisions. The decision-making process can be influenced by various factors, including but not limited to group size, dynamics, communication patterns, and power dynamics. The process of making decisions as a group can potentially reap benefits from a range of perspectives, yet it may also encounter obstacles such as conflicts, the establishment of consensus, and biases in decision-making.

Comprehending the circumstances that influence decision-making is of utmost importance for decision-makers to modify their methodology, procure pertinent data, and utilize appropriate decision-making methodologies. Effective decision-making may necessitate the implementation of specific strategies, utilization of analytical tools, or engagement of stakeholders, contingent upon varying conditions.

1.5 Role of Decision Making in Management

The process of making decisions holds significant importance in the realm of management, spanning various tiers of an enterprise. The function in question is a crucial aspect of management that has a significant impact on the efficacy, efficiency, and overall success of an organization. The following are essential functions of decision-making within the realm of management:

The process of decision making enables managers to establish the objectives and goals of the organization. During the process of decision-making, managers ascertain the objectives that require accomplishment and establish unambiguous goals for their respective teams. The process of making decisions serves to ensure that the actions of individuals and groups are in accordance with the overarching goals and objectives of the organization.

The process of planning and developing strategies involves a central focus on decision making. Organizational managers are responsible for making crucial decisions regarding the allocation of resources, market positioning, product development, and other factors that significantly influence the strategic direction of the organization. The implementation of proficient decision-making processes guarantees that proposed plans and strategies are thoroughly analyzed, practical, and in accordance with the goals of the organization.

Resource allocation is a critical managerial function that involves decision-making regarding the distribution of resources, such as financial, human, and material resources. The process of decision making entails the act of establishing priorities and making determinations regarding the allocation of resources to various projects, departments, or initiatives. The optimization of available resources and the support of organizational goals are facilitated by effective resource allocation decisions.

The process of making decisions is intricately connected to the act of problem-solving. The role of a manager is often fraught with challenges and obstacles, which necessitates the use of decision-making processes to effectively analyze problems, generate potential solutions, and ultimately select the most suitable course of action. The implementation of proficient problem-solving techniques via decision-making processes results in enhanced organizational efficiency, efficacy, and innovation.

The process of decision-making entails the evaluation of potential risks and uncertainties that are linked to various alternatives and implementing measures to mitigate them, which is commonly referred to as risk management. Managers engage in the process of risk identification, assessment of potential impact, and decision-making aimed at mitigating risks and optimizing rewards. The implementation of proficient risk management strategies via decision-making processes enables organizations to effectively navigate unpredictable circumstances and safeguard their interests.

The process of decision making plays a crucial role in promoting coordination and control within an organizational setting. Managers are responsible for making decisions pertaining to the coordination of activities, workflows, and processes within an organization. They establish the appropriate allocation of tasks, the optimal means of team collaboration, and the most effective flow of information. The process of decision making encompasses the activities of performance monitoring, outcome evaluation, and requisite adjustments to ensure the attainment of control and alignment with objectives[3].

Effective decision-making plays a pivotal role in promoting innovation and facilitating organizational adaptability. Organizational managers are responsible for making strategic decisions pertaining to the exploration of novel concepts, allocation of resources towards research and development, and adoption of transformative changes. The process of decision making empowers managers to undertake measured risks, foster imaginative ideation, and stimulate innovation across their teams and the entire organization.

Effective leadership entails decision-making as a crucial component that is closely intertwined with motivation. Leadership personnel engage in decision-making processes that stimulate and encourage their subordinates, furnishing them with guidance and orientation. Through the inclusion of employees in decision-making processes, managers are able to provide them with empowerment, cultivate a sense of ownership, and augment levels of employee engagement.

To summarize, the act of making decisions is a crucial aspect of the managerial role. This statement highlights that the process of planning, allocating resources, problem-solving, managing risks, coordinating activities, and controlling operations within an

[3] Simon, H. A. (1960). The New Science of Management Decision. Prentice Hall.

organization is guided by a particular framework. The ability to make effective decisions is a crucial skill for managers as it allows them to establish goals, foster creativity, and offer guidance, ultimately leading to the triumph and efficacy of the enterprise.

Chapter 2: The Decision Making Process

This chapter takes a deeper dive into the stages of the decision-making process. Decision making is not merely selecting a choice from available alternatives; it's a systematic process involving several stages.

2.1 Steps in Decision Making

The process of decision-making generally comprises a sequence of measures that assist individuals or groups in methodically examining a circumstance, assessing options, and selecting the optimal course of action.

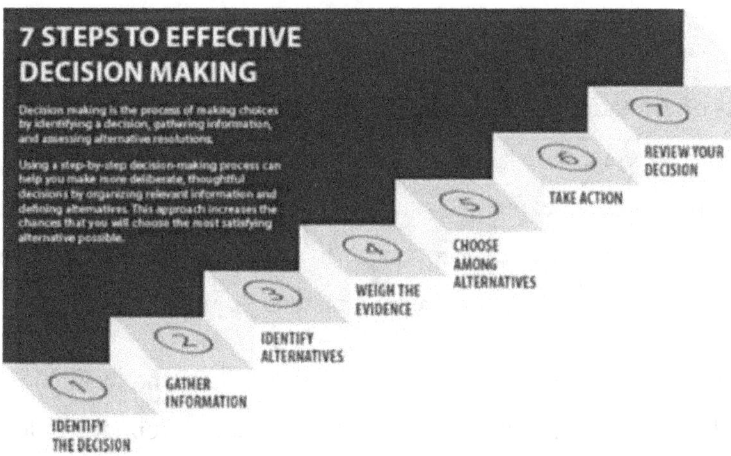

Source: UMass, Dartmouth, Decision-Making Process, 2023

Various models and frameworks have been proposed in the literature; however, the decision-making process typically involves the following fundamental steps:

The initial stage involves precisely identifying and defining the decision that necessitates resolution. This entails comprehending the issue or potentiality at stake and articulating it in a lucid and succinct fashion.

Acquire Pertinent Data: Upon determining the decision, procure all pertinent information that is requisite for making a well-informed selection. The process may entail the acquisition of data, execution of research, solicitation of expert perspectives, or referencing pertinent resources[4].

The initial step in the decision-making process is to identify alternatives by generating a variety of potential solutions or options. Generate a range of potential alternatives that possess the capacity to attain the intended results. It is crucial to take into account both traditional and novel options.

The process of evaluating alternatives involves the assessment and evaluation of each option against predetermined criteria or objectives. It is advisable to evaluate the merits, demerits, hazards, expenses, gains, and practicability of every alternative. This process may entail performing a cost-benefit evaluation, assessing advantages and disadvantages, or utilizing decision-making methodologies like decision matrices.

Reach a Conclusion: Following a thorough evaluation of the available alternatives, arrive at a decision by choosing the option that is most appropriate. Select the option that is consistent with the intended results, adequately tackles the issue or opportunity, and is substantiated by the accessible data and evaluation.

Upon reaching a decision, it is imperative to devise a comprehensive strategy for executing it. Identify the requisite measures, apportion resources, and set a schedule

[4] Mintzberg, H., Raisinghani, D., & Theoret, A. (1976). The Structure of Unstructured Decision Processes. Administrative Science Quarterly, 21(2), 246-275.

for implementation. Effectively convey the determination to pertinent stakeholders and guarantee their comprehension and dedication.

The process of monitoring and evaluating involves overseeing the execution of a decision and assessing its efficacy. Evaluate the results, gauge performance, and contrast the realized outcomes with the anticipated ones. This particular stage facilitates the identification of any deviations or modifications that may be necessary to attain the intended results.

Engage in the process of learning and enhancing one's abilities by reflecting on the decision-making process and its corresponding outcomes. Identify the key takeaways and opportunities for enhancement. Leverage this knowledge to optimize forthcoming decision-making processes and foster a culture of continuous learning within the organization.

It is noteworthy that the process of decision making is not invariably a linear progression, and certain stages may exhibit overlap or necessitate repetition. Moreover, the intricacy and importance of the decision could impact the degree of examination and engagement of stakeholders. Notwithstanding, adhering to these overarching procedures can assist individuals and entities in rendering more efficient and knowledgeable judgments.

2.2 Importance of Each Step

Every stage in the process of decision-making has a distinct objective and adds to the overall efficiency and triumph of the decision. Omitting or disregarding any stage in the decision-making process may result in adverse outcomes and undermine the decision's caliber. Let us briefly examine the significance of each step.

The act of precisely identifying the decision at hand serves to concentrate the decision-making process and guarantees that all parties involved possess a comprehensive comprehension of the problem or opportunity under consideration. This establishes the framework for acquiring pertinent data and formulating alternative solutions.

Acquiring pertinent information is of paramount importance in making well-informed decisions. The provision of pertinent facts, data, and insights facilitates comprehension of the situation, assessment of available options, and anticipation of potential consequences. Insufficient or deficient data may result in prejudiced or ill-informed decision-making.

The process of identifying alternatives involves generating a diverse set of options, which facilitates a thorough examination of possible solutions. The act of encouraging creative thinking has been found to broaden the perspective of decision makers, thereby increasing the likelihood of identifying innovative or optimal options.

The comprehensive evaluation of alternatives facilitates the assessment of their viability, benefits, drawbacks, and probable hazards. The process allows decision-makers to make objective comparisons and prioritize various options based on pertinent criteria and objectives. Conducting a thorough assessment guarantees that the chosen option is the most appropriate and consistent with the intended results.

The process of decision-making entails selecting the most appropriate option through a thorough assessment and analysis of available alternatives. This stage necessitates the contemplation of all pertinent variables, evaluating the pros and cons, and arriving at a judicious decision that is in line with the objectives and principles of the institution.

The implementation of a decision is a critical step in the process of transforming it into actionable outcomes. This stage entails formulating a comprehensive strategy, apportioning necessary resources, and disseminating the verdict to relevant parties. Efficient and effective execution of a decision is ensured through successful implementation.

The process of Monitoring and Evaluation involves the systematic tracking of the implementation of a decision and the assessment of its outcomes. This approach enables the determination of whether the decision has successfully achieved the intended results. The process furnishes an evaluation of the decision's efficacy, detects any divergences, and enables modifications or remedial actions as required.

The process of reflecting on the decision-making process and its outcomes is crucial for both learning and improvement. Through the identification of lessons learned, both organizations and individuals can improve their decision-making abilities, streamline their processes, and prevent the recurrence of errors in subsequent endeavors.

The decision-making process can be optimized by adhering to each step, which can lead to the reduction of biases, the exploration of a broader spectrum of options, the ability to make informed decisions, and an increase in the probability of achieving favorable outcomes.

2.3 Limitations and Challenges

The process of making decisions is not exempt from encountering limitations and challenges. The quality of decisions can be influenced by a multitude of factors and circumstances. The process of decision making is often accompanied by various limitations and challenges that are commonly encountered.

In many cases, decisions are made relying on the information that is accessible, which may be restricted, unclear, or indeterminate. Insufficient or imprecise data may result in decisions that are less than optimal.

Cognitive biases are a prevalent phenomenon among decision makers, characterized by systematic errors in thinking that have the potential to distort judgment and decision-making processes. Cognitive biases, such as confirmation bias, which involves the tendency to favor information that confirms pre-existing beliefs, and anchoring bias, which involves the over-reliance on initial information, have the potential to impede objective and rational decision-making processes.

The impact of emotions on decision-making processes can result in irrational decision-making. The decision-making process can be influenced by strong emotions such as fear, overconfidence, or personal biases, which can lead to impaired judgment[5].

The presence of temporal limitations can lead to expeditious or impulsive decision-making. The absence of adequate time allocated for comprehensive analysis and evaluation may result in the omission of crucial factors or alternatives.

The process of group decision making entails the management of interpersonal dynamics, diverse opinions, and power struggles within a group. Obstacles such as groupthink, which refers to the tendency to conform in order to avoid conflict, or information cascades, which involve adopting the opinions of others without engaging in critical evaluation, have the potential to impede the process of making sound decisions.

Excessive analysis or indecisiveness can hinder the process of making decisions. The pursuit of complete information or apprehension regarding erroneous decision-making may result in procrastination and lost prospects.

Numerous decisions entail inherent uncertainties and risks related to them. Accurately predicting future outcomes or assessing probabilities can pose a significant challenge. In certain scenarios, decision makers may be required to navigate a complex set of trade-offs between potential risks and rewards, despite the absence of complete certainty.

The process of implementing a decision may encounter challenges, despite the decision being well-informed and carefully considered. The successful implementation of decisions can be impeded by various factors such as resistance to change, resource limitations, or unanticipated challenges.

---

[5] Malhotra, N. K., & Birks, D. F. (2007). Marketing Research: An Applied Approach. Pearson Education.

Evaluation bias can impact the assessment of decisions post-implementation. The assessment of decision quality can be distorted by hindsight bias, which involves perceiving outcomes as predictable after the fact, or outcome bias, which entails evaluating decisions based on their outcomes rather than the decision-making process.

The presence of ethical dilemmas can pose challenges to the process of decision-making, thereby necessitating careful consideration of ethical considerations. The task of making decisions that are ethically sound can be challenging due to the need to reconcile competing interests, moral principles, and organizational values.

It is imperative for decision makers to possess an understanding of the constraints and obstacles at hand. The utilization of strategies to mitigate biases, the gathering of pertinent information, the consideration of multiple perspectives, and the critical evaluation of decisions are all beneficial in aiding individuals. Through recognition and resolution of these obstacles, policymakers can endeavor to achieve decision-making that is both more efficient and well-informed.

Chapter 3: Information Gathering

The third chapter in this series focuses on the second step of the decision-making process: gathering relevant information. Quality decisions require accurate, timely, and comprehensive information.

3.1 Importance of Information Gathering

The acquisition of data holds significant importance in the process of making informed decisions. The process entails the acquisition of pertinent information, empirical evidence, and discerning observations that serve as a basis for making well-informed decisions. The significance of gathering information can be comprehended by considering the subsequent factors:

Improved Comprehension: The act of collecting data enables individuals in positions of authority to acquire a thorough comprehension of the issue or potential benefit that is before them. This aids in the identification of crucial components, factors, and variables, thereby facilitating a more precise evaluation of the circumstances.

The process of making informed decisions relies on the availability and utilization of relevant information. Through the acquisition of pertinent data and insights, individuals in positions of authority can effectively analyze various alternatives, evaluate potential hazards and benefits, and ultimately ascertain the optimal path forward. Making informed decisions increases the likelihood of achieving favorable results.

The act of gathering information serves to decrease uncertainty by offering a clearer understanding of present circumstances, potential consequences, and corresponding hazards. The utilization of scenario analysis enables decision makers to evaluate the probability and ramifications of various potential outcomes, thereby facilitating the process of making informed and assured decisions.

The process of gathering information facilitates the assessment and juxtaposition of options. The process assists decision-makers in collecting information regarding various alternatives, evaluating their advantages and disadvantages, and comprehending the potential advantages and disadvantages of each option. This enables a more thorough and impartial process of making decisions.

The process of gathering information can facilitate the identification of patterns, trends, and correlations that may not be immediately evident. Through the process of data analysis and information gathering, decision-makers can effectively recognize emerging trends, market dynamics, customer preferences, and other pertinent factors that may significantly impact decision-making outcomes.

The process of gathering information enables decision makers to verify their assumptions and experiment with their hypotheses. Decision makers can ensure the accuracy and currency of their decisions by seeking pertinent data and facts, instead of relying exclusively on subjective beliefs or biases.

The process of stakeholder engagement entails the active involvement of relevant parties in order to obtain their viewpoints, knowledge, and proficiency. This is done through information gathering. Collaboration is encouraged, a common comprehension of the decision context is nurtured, and decision makers are enabled to contemplate a range of perspectives. The adoption of an inclusive approach has the potential to result in improved decision-making outcomes and heightened stakeholder support.

The process of risk management is facilitated by the acquisition of pertinent information. Through the process of gathering and scrutinizing pertinent data, individuals in positions of authority can discern possible hazards, evaluate their potential consequences and probability, and formulate tactics to alleviate or control them. This facilitates proactive decision-making and diminishes the likelihood of unforeseen setbacks.

To summarize, the process of gathering information is of paramount importance in order to make well-informed decisions. Data analysis serves to improve comprehension, reduce ambiguity, streamline the assessment of options, detect regularities and tendencies, verify presuppositions, involve interested parties, and bolster risk mitigation efforts. Decision makers can enhance the accuracy, effectiveness, and success of their decisions by dedicating time and effort to comprehensive information gathering.

3.2 Types of Information Sources

There are many different kinds of information sources available for learning things and doing research. The aforementioned sources can be classified into three distinct categories, namely primary sources, secondary sources, and tertiary sources. The following categories will be examined in detail:

Primary sources refer to the original materials or firsthand accounts that provide information about an event or research. Primary sources offer firsthand information or empirical data and are usually authored by individuals who directly observed or participated in the events or phenomena being studied. Primary sources are exemplified by:

Empirical investigations and experimental inquiries.

The collection of data through interviews and surveys.

Diaries, letters, and personal correspondence are forms of written communication that are typically used for personal expression or communication between individuals.

Oral presentations and historical accounts conveyed through spoken words.

Official reports and government documents.

Artifacts and objects are two distinct categories of material culture.

Primary sources hold significant value in providing insights into particular events or phenomena, and they are frequently employed in historical investigations or scientific inquiries.

Secondary sources are produced through the process of synthesizing or analyzing primary sources. Academic discourse involves the provision of interpretations, evaluations, or summaries of primary information. Secondary sources are commonly authored by individuals who were not directly involved in the events they are documenting. Secondary sources are exemplified by:

Literary works and educational materials in print format.

Review articles are a type of academic literature that provide a comprehensive analysis and synthesis of existing research on a particular topic. They are typically written by experts in the field and aim to provide readers with a critical evaluation of the current state of knowledge on the topic. Review articles can be useful for researchers who are looking to gain a deeper understanding of a particular area of study, as well as for practitioners who are seeking to stay up-to-date with the latest developments in their field.

Biographies

Literary critiques refer to the evaluation and analysis of literary works, typically conducted by scholars or experts in the field.

Documentary films are non-fictional motion pictures that aim to inform or educate viewers about real-life events, people, or issues. They often employ various techniques such as interviews, archival footage, and reenactments to present a factual account of the subject matter. Documentary films can cover a wide range of topics, from social and political issues to historical events and scientific discoveries. They are often used as a tool for advocacy, education, and social change.

News articles that offer analysis or commentary.

Secondary sources are valuable resources for obtaining a comprehensive perspective or comprehending the contextual background of a subject matter. Frequently, a more comprehensive viewpoint is offered through the amalgamation of various primary sources or the integration of pre-existing research.

Tertiary sources are a type of information resource that collates and arranges data obtained from primary and secondary sources. They provide abridged synopses or uncomplicated elucidations of intricate subjects. Tertiary sources are commonly produced to facilitate expeditious consultation or provide fundamental information. Tertiary sources are exemplified by:

Encyclopedias Dictionaries

Guidebooks

Handbooks Almanacs

Online platforms such as Wikipedia, despite their potential inclusion of both secondary and tertiary sources of information, are commonly utilized by individuals seeking knowledge on a particular subject.

Tertiary sources serve as valuable resources for obtaining concise information or gaining a broad comprehension of a topic. Nonetheless, tertiary sources may not exhibit the same level of specificity or comprehensiveness as primary or secondary sources.

It is imperative to acknowledge that the dependability and precision of data may fluctuate among diverse sources. When engaging in research, it is recommended to take into account the reliability, proficiency, and partiality of the source in order to ascertain the veracity of the information.

3.3 Data Collection Methods

Data collection methods pertain to the methodologies and protocols employed in procuring data and information for the purposes of research or analysis. The selection of methods may exhibit variability contingent upon the research inquiry's characteristics, the resources at hand, and the intended results. The following are frequently employed techniques for gathering data:

Surveys are a data collection method that employs questionnaires or interviews to gather information from a subset of individuals. Surveys can be administered via various modes such as face-to-face interviews, telephone conversations, postal mail, or online platforms. Surveys are a valuable tool for collecting both quantitative and qualitative data pertaining to individuals' opinions, behaviors, and attitudes.

Interviews are a method of data collection that entails face-to-face discussions between the researcher and the participant. The questionnaires can be categorized into three types, namely structured, semi-structured, and unstructured, based on the degree of flexibility allowed in the questioning process. Interviews are a valuable method for gathering comprehensive qualitative data and obtaining insights from participants.

Observations refer to the methodical process of observing and documenting behaviors, occurrences, or phenomena in their authentic surroundings. This approach has the potential to collect qualitative data pertaining to human conduct, social exchanges, or natural occurrences. Empirical data can be collected through either participant-based research, where the researcher is actively involved, or non-participant-based research, where the researcher acts solely as an observer.

Experiments refer to systematic and controlled procedures that involve the manipulation of variables and the observation of their effects. Establishing cause-and-effect relationships is a frequent application of these in scientific research. Empirical investigations can be carried out either within controlled laboratory conditions or in naturalistic field settings.

Case studies entail a comprehensive examination of a specific individual, group, organization, or situation. Commonly, they encompass a variety of techniques for gathering data, including but not limited to interviews, observations, and document analysis. Case studies offer comprehensive and situation-specific perspectives.

The process of document analysis entails scrutinizing and construing written, visual, or audio materials. This approach involves scrutinizing extant documents, records, reports, archival data, media sources, and other types of recorded information. The practice of scrutinizing documents is a widely employed method in the fields of historical inquiry, content analysis, and textual interpretation.

The research methodology of focus groups entails the assembly of a limited number of participants to engage in a guided discussion on a particular subject matter, facilitated by a moderator. The group's interactions and discussions yield qualitative data pertaining to collective perceptions, opinions, and experiences.

Ethnography is a research methodology that entails complete involvement in a specific social or cultural environment to meticulously record and analyze the customary practices, conduct, and social exchanges of the individuals within that milieu. Ethnographic inquiry frequently integrates participant observation, interviews, and document analysis to furnish a comprehensive comprehension of a particular social group or community[6].

The process of secondary data analysis entails the utilization of pre-existing data that was originally gathered for a different research objective. Scholars scrutinize and construe the aforementioned data to address novel research inquiries. Secondary data sources encompass a variety of materials, such as publicly accessible datasets, government records, academic databases, and organizational records.

---

[6] Davenport, T. H., & Harris, J. G. (2007). Competing on Analytics: The New Science of Winning. Harvard Business School Press.

The selection of suitable data collection methods is a crucial aspect that must be considered in accordance with the research objectives, the target population, and the available resources. Scholars frequently utilize a variety of methodologies in order to augment the credibility and dependability of their results.

3.4 Role of Business Intelligence and Analytics in Decision Making

The utilization of Business Intelligence (BI) and analytics is of paramount importance in the decision-making procedures of enterprises. The process entails gathering, scrutinizing, and construing data to furnish practical discernments and facilitate strategic decision-making. The utilization of business intelligence and analytics plays a crucial role in the process of decision making. Some of the significant functions of these tools include:

The utilization of Business Intelligence (BI) and analytics empowers organizations to make decisions based on empirical data, rather than relying solely on subjective intuition or instinctual reactions. Through the utilization of data and analytics tools, decision-makers can acquire a comprehensive comprehension of their business operations, customer behavior, market trends, and other pertinent factors. The utilization of a data-driven approach has been shown to mitigate biases and enhance the likelihood of rendering well-informed and efficacious decisions.

The utilization of business intelligence (BI) and analytics enables organizations to effectively monitor and measure crucial performance indicators (KPIs) and metrics. These instruments facilitate the monitoring of the efficacy of diverse organizational procedures, units, commodities, or amenities by individuals responsible for making decisions. Organizations can conduct performance analysis by scrutinizing data in real-time or over specific timeframes to pinpoint areas that require improvement, evaluate the consequences of decisions, and implement remedial measures as necessary.

Business intelligence and analytics tools employ sophisticated methodologies, including predictive and prescriptive analytics, to enhance their analytical capabilities. Predictive analytics is a methodology that leverages past data and statistical models to anticipate forthcoming patterns, actions, or consequences. This facilitates the ability of organizations to forecast customer requirements, fluctuations in the market, and potential risks. Prescriptive analytics surpasses mere outcome prediction by offering practical recommendations to enhance decision-making. These instruments facilitate proactive decision-making and enable organizations to capitalize on opportunities before they materialize.

Business Intelligence (BI) and analytics have the potential to provide organizations with significant insights into their target market and customer base. Through the examination of customer data, encompassing preferences, purchasing behaviors, and feedback, corporations can acquire a more comprehensive comprehension of their customers' requirements and anticipations. The aforementioned insights have the potential to provide direction for product development, marketing strategies, and customer relationship management. Consequently, they can facilitate more efficient decision-making in domains such as product launches, pricing, promotions, and customer experience enhancements.

The utilization of business intelligence and analytics by organizations can confer a competitive advantage by facilitating the identification of market trends, monitoring of competitors, and discovery of latent opportunities. Through the examination of both internal and external data, entities can conduct a SWOT analysis to ascertain their strengths, weaknesses, opportunities, and threats. This process enables them to develop efficacious strategies and allocate resources optimally. Business intelligence (BI) and analytics tools play a crucial role in enabling organizations to conduct scenario planning, risk assessments, and strategic decision-making processes, thereby augmenting their overall competitiveness.

Business Intelligence (BI) and analytics have been identified as effective tools for enhancing operational efficiency and cost optimization within organizations. Through the examination of operational data, entities can detect hindrances, inadequacies, and zones that require process enhancement. The utilization of a data-centric methodology enables individuals in positions of authority to make well-informed decisions pertaining to the allocation of resources, management of supply chains, optimization of inventory, and streamlining of operations. Through the implementation of cost reduction strategies and efficiency enhancement measures, organizations can attain greater levels of profitability and sustainability.

In general, the utilization of business intelligence and analytics provides decision-makers with precise, prompt, and pertinent data, which facilitates their ability to arrive at well-informed judgments that propel the success of the organization. Through the utilization of data-driven insights, entities can enhance their operational efficiency, recognize avenues for expansion, alleviate potential hazards, and maintain a competitive edge in a progressively data-oriented commercial environment.

Chapter 4: Decision Analysis

This chapter delves into the analysis phase of the decision-making process. Once relevant information has been collected, decision-makers need to make sense of it. Decision analysis involves using various tools and techniques to evaluate possible choices.

4.1 Tools and Techniques for Decision Analysis

The process of decision analysis entails a methodical approach to arriving at well-informed decisions through the consideration of multiple alternatives, the assessment of potential outcomes, and the integration of uncertainties or risks. Various methodologies and instruments can be employed to facilitate the process of decision analysis. The following are frequently utilized.

Decision trees are visual tools that depict various decision alternatives, potential consequences, and their corresponding probabilities or values. These tools facilitate the visualization and analysis of decision scenarios that involve multiple branches and potential consequences. Decision trees are a valuable tool for evaluating various options, estimating anticipated outcomes, and evaluating the effects of uncertainties.

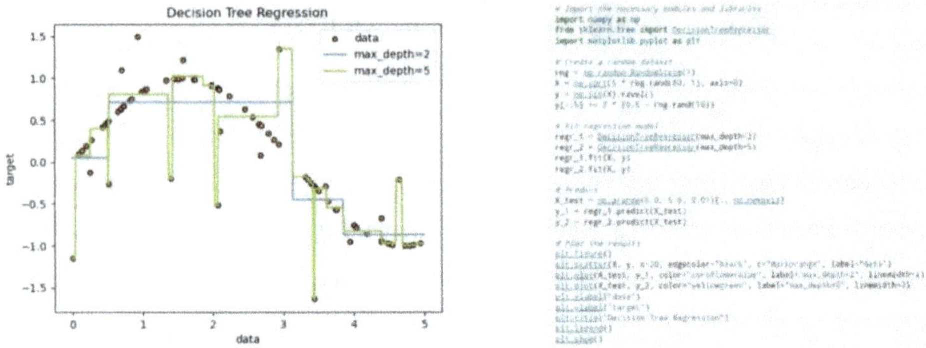

Source: Scikit Learn, Decision tree regression

Influence diagrams are visual aids that depict the interconnections between various factors, choices, risks, and consequences. Decision trees offer a systematic depiction of decision-making scenarios, facilitating the recognition of crucial variables and interrelationships. In the realm of decision analysis, influence diagrams serve as a valuable tool for comprehending causal relationships, as well as for quantifying probabilities or values, and assessing decision strategies.

The Monte Carlo Simulation is a computational technique that involves the generation of multiple iterations or simulations based on probabilistic models to estimate the range of possible outcomes and their respective probabilities. The methodology involves the integration of stochastic elements, such as uncertainties and random variables, to evaluate the probability of various outcomes. The utilization of Monte Carlo simulation offers a numerical methodology for decision analysis, enabling decision-makers to comprehend the possible hazards and arrive at well-informed decisions.

Sensitivity analysis is a method used to evaluate the impact of variations in input variables or parameters on the output or outcome of a decision model. This aids in the identification of the most significant factors and the evaluation of their influence on the decision-making process. Decision-makers can enhance their comprehension of the resilience of their decisions and obtain valuable insights into crucial areas that may necessitate additional analysis by manipulating key variables within a specified range.

Decision matrices, which are also referred to as decision grids or decision tables, are systematic instruments that facilitate the comparison and assessment of alternatives by taking into account various criteria or factors. Decision-makers are enabled to allocate weights or significance values to diverse criteria and assess alternatives correspondingly. The utilization of decision matrices offers a methodical and lucid approach to evaluate and contrast alternatives, thereby promoting impartial decision-making.

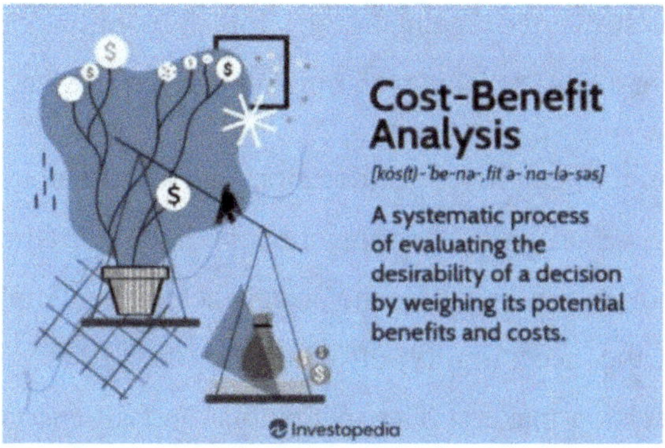

Source: Adam Hayes, What is Cost-Benefit Analysis, how is it used, what are its pros and cons?,Investopedia, 2023, Adapted from Michela Buttignol / Investopedia

Cost-benefit analysis is a method that evaluates the costs and benefits associated with various alternatives in order to ascertain their relative attractiveness. The process entails the measurement and comparison of both financial and non-financial variables in order to evaluate the economic feasibility and comprehensive worth of various alternatives. The utilization of cost-benefit analysis enables decision-makers to evaluate the pros and cons of different options in order to determine the most advantageous course of action.

Scenario analysis is a method that entails the creation and assessment of various conceivable future scenarios, which are based on diverse assumptions and uncertainties. This facilitates the process of decision-making by enabling decision-makers to examine and evaluate a variety of potential consequences. Through the consideration of diverse scenarios, decision-makers can proactively anticipate potential risks, formulate contingency plans, and arrive at decisions that are resilient and flexible in the face of varying circumstances.

Multi-Criteria Decision Analysis (MCDA)[7] is a theoretical construct that integrates diverse decision criteria and their respective significance to assess and prioritize alternatives. Mathematical models and techniques are utilized to incorporate a variety of factors and the preferences of stakeholders. Multi-Criteria Decision Analysis (MCDA) offers a structured methodology for decision-making that involves a systematic process of evaluating and weighing multiple criteria to achieve a consensus.

The tools and techniques employed for decision analysis are not necessarily mutually exclusive and may be utilized in conjunction with one another. The selection of decision-making tools is contingent upon various factors, including the intricacy of the decision problem, the accessibility of data, the degree of uncertainty, and the predilections of decision-makers. The meticulous and all-encompassing process of decision analysis necessitates the careful selection and application of suitable tools and techniques.

4.2 Multi-Criteria Decision Making Methods

MCDM techniques are utilized to aid decision-makers in assessing and ranking alternatives while taking into account numerous criteria or objectives. The aforementioned techniques aid in organizing intricate decision-making scenarios and taking into account multiple variables concurrently. The following are frequently utilized Multiple Criteria Decision Making (MCDM) techniques:

The Analytic Hierarchy Process (AHP) is a frequently employed Multiple Criteria Decision Making (MCDM) technique that was formulated by Thomas Saaty. The

[7] Keeney, R. L., & Raiffa, H. (1976). Decisions with Multiple Objectives: Preferences and Value Tradeoffs. Wiley.

process entails decomposing a decision-making problem into a structured arrangement of criteria and options, and subsequently evaluating the relative merits of each option against each criterion through pairwise comparisons. Numerical scales are utilized by decision-makers to assign subjective judgments or preferences, which are subsequently synthesized to determine priority weights. The Analytic Hierarchy Process (AHP) facilitates the process of assigning numerical values and prioritizing options by considering the comparative significance of various criteria.

The Technique for Order of Preference by Similarity to Ideal Solution (TOPSIS) is a method used in decision-making processes. The TOPSIS technique is a comparative approach that evaluates alternatives in relation to both ideal and anti-ideal solutions. The method computes the proximity of each option to the aforementioned solutions by evaluating their spatial separation in a multi-dimensional domain delineated by criteria. The alternative that exhibits the minimum distance to the ideal solution and the maximum distance to the anti-ideal solution is regarded as the most favored.

The Preference Ranking Organization Method for Enrichment Evaluations (PROMETHEE) is a set of techniques that take into account various criteria to prioritize alternatives. The process entails conducting comparisons between pairs and subsequently aggregating criteria through the utilization of preference functions. The PROMETHEE techniques offer rankings that rely on net outranking flows, which consider both positive and negative criteria, along with varying preference thresholds.

The ELECTRE (Elimination and Choice Translating Reality) Methods are a group of Multiple Criteria Decision Making (MCDM) techniques that take into account binary outranking relations among alternatives. The utilization of pairwise comparisons and concordance/discordance measures is employed to assess alternatives in relation to decision criteria. The utilization of ELECTRE techniques facilitates the production of rankings and the categorization of alternatives into preference categories.

The Weighted Sum Model (WSM) is a straightforward and comprehensible Multiple Criteria Decision Making (MCDM) technique that entails assigning weights to criteria and consolidating scores or evaluations for alternatives. In the decision-making process, criteria are assigned weights according to their respective levels of significance, after which a weighted sum is computed for each alternative. The option that obtains the greatest cumulative score is regarded as the most favored.

Grey Relational Analysis (GRA) is a technique that is utilized to address decision-making issues that are characterized by restricted or ambiguous data. The grey relational coefficient is computed by evaluating the performance of various alternatives against a reference alternative across multiple criteria. The use of Grey Relational Analysis (GRA) facilitates the process of evaluating and ranking various alternatives by measuring their relative proximity to a reference alternative.

Data Envelopment Analysis (DEA) is a non-parametric technique that is utilized to assess the relative efficiency of various alternatives that possess multiple inputs and outputs. The process involves a comparative analysis of various options to determine their respective efficiencies, with a view to identifying the most optimal alternative. Additionally, it offers valuable insights into the potential enhancements that can be made to less efficient alternatives.

Fuzzy Set Theory is a mathematical framework utilized to manage imprecise or uncertain data and preferences. The utilization of linguistic terms or fuzzy numbers enables decision-makers to articulate their subjective judgments. Fuzzy Multiple Criteria Decision Making (MCDM) techniques integrate fuzzy logic and decision analysis methodologies to assess and prioritize various alternatives.

The selection of a Multiple Criteria Decision Making (MCDM) technique is contingent upon the particular decision-making scenario, the characteristics of the criteria and alternatives, and the inclinations of the decision-makers. It is imperative to take into account the strengths, limitations, and underlying assumptions of each methodology and opt for the most appropriate approach in accordance with the specific context.

4.3 Role of Data Analysis and Modeling in Decision Making

The utilization of data analysis and modeling is of utmost importance in the process of decision making, as it facilitates the provision of valuable insights, predictions, and simulations that aid in making informed choices. Data analysis and modeling play crucial roles in decision making by providing valuable insights and predictions based on the available data.

The process of data analysis enables decision-makers to obtain a thorough comprehension of the present circumstances. Through the examination of pertinent data sets, entities can discern trends, patterns, and correlations within their business activities, market circumstances, consumer conduct, and other crucial variables. This information aids in the evaluation of the advantages, disadvantages, prospects, and risks, empowering decision-makers to arrive at conclusions grounded in a comprehensive comprehension of the current circumstances.

The process of data analysis facilitates the identification of prospective opportunities and risks. Through the analysis of historical data, market trends, and customer preferences, organizations can discern nascent trends, market voids, or unaddressed customer demands[8]. This data assists stakeholders in recognizing novel commercial prospects and formulating tactics to exploit them. Data analysis enables organizations to evaluate and alleviate risks by detecting potential threats or vulnerabilities through the use of historical data or predictive analytics.

Data analysis is a valuable tool for decision-makers as it offers evidence-based insights to support their decision-making process. Through the process of data analysis and report generation, organizations are able to conduct objective evaluations of various alternatives, make comparisons between options, and assess the potential outcomes. The utilization of data analysis enables decision-makers to shift from subjective or

[8] Khan, S. A., & Zafar, M. W. (2013). Multi-Criteria Decision Making: A Comparative Study. International Journal of Operations Research and Information Systems, 4(4), 15-29.

intuitive decision-making approaches towards evidence-based information and quantitative analysis to facilitate informed decision-making.

The utilization of data analysis and modeling techniques facilitates the ability of organizations to forecast potential outcomes and future trends. Organizations can utilize statistical techniques, machine learning algorithms, or time series analysis to make predictions about customer demand, sales figures, market conditions, and other relevant variables. Forecasts aid in enabling decision-makers to anticipate forthcoming situations, strategize accordingly, and take proactive measures to attain a competitive advantage.

The optimization of decision-making processes can be facilitated through the utilization of data analysis, which can provide valuable insights into the most efficient strategies or approaches. By means of data-centric analysis, entities can pinpoint crucial performance metrics, gauge performance levels, and oversee advancement towards objectives. This data enables decision-makers to assess the efficacy of various decisions or strategies, implement modifications as necessary, and consistently enhance decision-making procedures.

Modeling and simulation techniques enable decision-makers to evaluate various scenarios and their potential consequences prior to making decisions. This process involves simulating and testing different scenarios to determine their impact. Organizations can employ modeling techniques to simulate different alternatives and manipulate significant variables, thereby facilitating an analysis of potential outcomes, comprehension of trade-offs, and informed decision-making. This methodology aids in mitigating ambiguity and improving the caliber of judgments by taking into account various scenarios and their corresponding hazards.

The processes of strategic planning and resource allocation are facilitated by data analysis and modeling. Through the examination of past records, evaluation of market patterns, and assessment of rival accomplishments, corporations can ascertain strategic imperatives, efficiently distribute resources, and establish realistic objectives. The process of analyzing data facilitates the ability of decision-makers to make informed and evidence-based decisions regarding the allocation of resources, investments, and prioritization. This approach ensures that the decisions made are in line with the overall objectives of the organization.

In general, the utilization of data analysis and modeling offers decision-makers a robust basis of understanding and perspectives. Through the utilization of data, entities can make well-informed judgments, anticipate results, enhance procedures, and efficiently distribute resources. In contemporary times, the significance of data analysis and modeling in the process of decision-making has escalated for enterprises striving to maintain their competitiveness and accomplish their objectives in a data-centric environment.

Chapter 5: Decision Making Models

This chapter focuses on different models of decision making that provide frameworks to understand how decisions are made. These models can help identify the most effective strategies for making better decisions.

5.1 Prescriptive (Rational) Decision Making Model

The prescriptive decision-making model, commonly referred to as the rational decision-making model, is a methodical framework that directs decision-makers in making optimal selections through the application of logic and reasoning. The procedure adheres to a methodical approach that encompasses multiple stages. The prescriptive decision-making model comprises several essential steps that are crucial to the decision-making process.

The initial stage involves the identification and definition of the problem or decision to be made. The process entails acknowledging the disparity between the present circumstances and the intended outcome, while also comprehending the fundamental reasons and ramifications of the issue.

In the context of decision-making, it is imperative to establish precise and unambiguous objectives subsequent to identifying the issue at hand. This process is commonly referred to as goal setting. Objectives establish the intended results and offer a structure for assessing different approaches. The utilization of SMART (specific, measurable, achievable, relevant, and time-bound) goals is beneficial in providing direction for the decision-making process.

During the "Generating Alternatives" phase, individuals responsible for making decisions engage in a process of ideation to produce a variety of potential alternatives or solutions aimed at resolving the problem that has been identified. It is imperative to contemplate a wide range of options and engage in innovative thinking to guarantee a thorough examination of alternatives.

The subsequent stage entails the assessment and scrutiny of the feasible alternatives in light of the predetermined objectives and standards. Decision-makers evaluate the benefits, drawbacks, and potential consequences of each option. The process of evaluation frequently entails the collection of pertinent data, execution of analysis, and utilization of decision analysis instruments such as decision matrices, cost-benefit analysis, or decision trees to measure and contrast the available options.

Decision selection involves the careful evaluation of available alternatives, followed by the selection of the most suitable option that is consistent with the established goals and criteria[9]. This stage entails evaluating the pros and cons of every option, taking into account any potential trade-offs, and analyzing the potential risks and uncertainties linked to each decision.

Execution: Following the decision-making process, the subsequent step involves the efficient implementation of the chosen course of action. The process entails formulating a course of action, distributing resources, delegating tasks, and establishing a schedule for implementation. The successful execution of a decision necessitates precise communication, coordination, and monitoring to guarantee its effectiveness.

The ultimate stage entails the assessment and provision of feedback on the results of the decision-making process. The evaluative process undertaken by decision-makers involves an assessment of the efficacy of the selected alternative, an evaluation of its impact on the problem at hand, and a comparison of the achieved outcomes with the intended objectives. The feedback garnered from the process of evaluation can serve

[9] March, J. G. (1994). A Primer on Decision Making: How Decisions Happen. The Free Press.

as a valuable resource for informing future decision-making processes and refining the decision-making model.

The prescriptive model of decision-making postulates that decision-makers possess comprehensive information, utilize rationality in their decision-making process, and strive to optimize their choices to attain the most favorable outcome. It is crucial to recognize that decision-making in practical settings frequently encompasses factors such as incomplete information, uncertainties, and cognitive biases. It may be imperative to make modifications to the prescriptive model, such as integrating intuition or tackling bounded rationality, in order to accommodate these intricacies and enhance the efficacy of decision-making.

5.2 Descriptive (Behavioral) Decision Making Model

The descriptive decision-making model, also referred to as the behavioral decision-making model, centers on the depiction and comprehension of how individuals and groups effectively arrive at decisions, as opposed to dictating how they ought to make decisions. The statement acknowledges that the process of decision-making is susceptible to the influence of cognitive biases, heuristics, emotions, and other behavioral factors. The descriptive decision-making model comprises several essential constituents, which include:

The concept of bounded rationality posits that decision-makers possess restricted cognitive capacities and information processing capabilities, as described by the descriptive model. According to the concept of bounded rationality, individuals have a tendency to opt for decisions that are satisfactory or deemed "good enough" instead of striving for the most optimal solution. Decision-makers often employ heuristics and simplifying strategies as a means of managing intricate decision problems and cognitive constraints.

Cognitive biases refer to consistent and predictable patterns of deviation from rationality that occur during the process of decision-making. The descriptive model acknowledges the impact of various biases, including confirmation bias, availability bias, and anchoring bias. Confirmation bias refers to the tendency to favor information that aligns with pre-existing beliefs, while availability bias involves relying on easily accessible information. Anchoring bias, on the other hand, pertains to the influence of initial information on subsequent decision-making. The presence of biases has the potential to affect the caliber and impartiality of decision-making.

The decision context and framing are crucial factors that exert a considerable influence on the process of decision-making. The presentation or framing of a decision problem has the potential to exert an influence on the choices that are ultimately made. Individuals may display varying preferences or proclivities towards risk-taking contingent upon whether a given scenario is presented as a prospective gain or a prospective loss. The significance of contextual and framing effects on decision outcomes is underscored by the descriptive model.

The descriptive model acknowledges that decision-making is not exclusively a rational and logical process, but also involves intuition and emotions. Decision-making is also influenced by intuition, gut feelings, and emotions. Judgments and choices can be influenced by emotional states, personal values, and past experiences. Intuitive decision-making is a cognitive process that entails drawing upon unconscious mechanisms and heuristics to swiftly arrive at decisions by discerning patterns or cues.

The descriptive model recognizes that social factors can exert an influence on decision-making. The decision-making processes of a group, adherence to social norms, and conformity can exert a significant influence on the choices made by individuals. The phenomenon of social conformity or the inclination to preserve group harmony may exert an impact on the decision-making process of individuals in positions of authority. This influence may stem from the opinions and actions of others.

The descriptive model acknowledges that the process of decision-making can be influenced by an individual's learning and experience. Both individuals and organizations have the capacity to derive insights from prior decisions and outcomes, which may subsequently impact their future decision-making processes. The acquisition of experience can facilitate the cultivation of proficiency and intuition, thereby empowering individuals to make decisions that are better informed and more expedient.

The descriptive decision-making model aids in elucidating and forecasting decision-making behaviors by comprehending and depicting the actual process of decision-making. This statement offers valuable insights into the various factors that can influence decision outcomes, including biases, heuristics, and social influences. The acquisition of this knowledge can prove to be advantageous in the enhancement of decision-making efficacy through the reduction of biases and the implementation of interventions aimed at improving decision-making processes.

5.3 Intuition and Decision Making

Intuition is defined as the capacity to comprehend or apprehend something spontaneously without depending on explicit reasoning or conscious analysis. Intuitive decision-making, characterized by its swift, involuntary, and reflexive nature, can exert a substantial influence on the decision-making process. The following are salient aspects pertaining to intuition and its function in the process of decision making:

Intuitive decision-making is distinguished by its rapidity and automatic nature. The process entails expeditiously forming assessments or decisions relying on patterns, prior encounters, or intuition, frequently without deliberate consciousness or explicit justification.

Proficiency and Background: Intuition exhibits a strong correlation with proficiency and background knowledge. Professionals who specialize in a specific field frequently acquire robust intuition over time as a result of extensive experience and exposure to diverse circumstances. Individuals develop a profound comprehension of the topic, which facilitates their ability to swiftly and precisely assess situations based on their amassed expertise and recognition of patterns.

The process of intuition is predicated on the ability to recognize patterns, wherein decision-makers identify familiar patterns or resemblances between the present circumstances and their prior encounters. They utilize their pattern recognition abilities to swiftly evaluate and make decisions.

Non-conscious processing is involved in intuitive decision-making, which takes place at a level that is not consciously accessible. The cognitive mechanism underlying intuition occurs at a subconscious level, rendering it arduous to verbalize or elucidate the rationale behind intuitive judgments.

Emotional and implicit factors have the potential to impact intuition, as it may be susceptible to the influence of biases that are not consciously recognized. The affective domain can serve as a guiding force for decision-makers, leading them towards options that are congruent with their emotional state or that evoke a sense of subjective rightness. Intuitive judgments and choices can be influenced by implicit biases, which are shaped by cultural or personal beliefs.

Intuition is regarded as a complementary aspect to analytical thinking, rather than a mutually exclusive one, as it serves to enhance and supplement the latter. Analytical decision-making is predicated on deliberate analysis, methodical reasoning, and the careful consideration of advantages and disadvantages. However, in situations that are intricate or time-sensitive, intuition can furnish decision-makers with valuable insights and serve as a guiding force.

The precision of intuition may fluctuate contingent upon the contextual factors and the decision-maker's level of acquaintance with the circumstance. In situations that are familiar or routine, decision-makers with extensive experience and expertise tend to rely more on their intuition, which is perceived to be more dependable. In intricate or novel circumstances, intuition may exhibit reduced accuracy and susceptibility to biases.

Validation and calibration are crucial in ensuring the accuracy and reliability of intuitive decisions. Although intuition can offer valuable insights, it is imperative to subject intuitive judgments to testing and validation against existing data, analytical reasoning, or alternative perspectives to ensure precision and mitigate biases.

The cultivation of intuition can be achieved through purposeful training, exposure to a range of circumstances, and introspective contemplation. Decision-makers can improve their intuitive abilities by proactively soliciting feedback, engaging in reflective thinking about past decisions, and intentionally learning from their experiences.

It is noteworthy that although intuition may hold value in the process of decision-making, it is not invariably reliable [10]. The phenomenon under consideration may be susceptible to various forms of partiality, inaccuracies, and erroneous assessments. Thus, an equitable strategy that integrates intuition alongside analytical thinking, data analysis, and methodical reasoning can result in more resilient and knowledgeable decision-making consequences.

---

[10] Klein, G. (2008). Naturalistic Decision Making. Human Factors, 50(3), 456-460.

Chapter 6: Group Decision Making

This chapter focuses on the process and dynamics of group decision making. While individual decision making is often quicker and more straightforward, group decision making is an integral part of most organizational settings and can lead to more effective decisions.

6.1 Advantages and Disadvantages of Group Decision Making

The process of making decisions as a group entails the collaborative involvement of several individuals. Although group decision making has various potential benefits, it also entails certain drawbacks. The purpose of this discourse is to examine the merits and demerits of group decision making.

The benefits of making decisions in a group setting.

The utilization of group decision making facilitates the incorporation of a variety of perspectives, experiences, and expertise, thereby promoting diversity. Diverse individuals possess distinct knowledge and perspectives that can lead to a more exhaustive examination of the issue and a broader spectrum of feasible remedies.

Group settings have been observed to promote creativity and innovation. The collaborative engagement and dissemination of thoughts within a group can incite innovative ideas and produce original resolutions that may have eluded solitary efforts. Collaborative ideation sessions, specifically in a group setting, have the potential to yield a higher quantity of innovative concepts.

Group decision making can improve problem-solving abilities by involving multiple individuals. The members of a group have the ability to offer diverse perspectives in analyzing a problem, recognizing possible hazards or disadvantages, and presenting alternative viewpoints. Collaborative endeavors have the potential to yield stronger and more efficient solutions to problems.

Enhancement of Decision Quality: The process of group decision making has the potential to improve decision quality through the reduction of individual biases and errors. By means of discourse and deliberation, members of a group can question one another's presumptions, exchange knowledge, and conduct a more comprehensive assessment of alternatives[11]. The process of collaboration has the potential to result in decisions that are more comprehensive and knowledgeable.

The involvement of group members in the decision-making process has been found to have a positive impact on their level of ownership, commitment, and acceptance of the ultimate decision. When individuals perceive that their viewpoints are acknowledged and esteemed, they are more inclined to endorse and proactively execute the selected plan of action.

The drawbacks associated with group decision making.

Group decision making can be a process that requires a significant amount of time. The attainment of a consensus or agreement may necessitate protracted deliberations, potentially leading to time lags, particularly in the context of sizable or heterogeneous cohorts.

Groupthink is a phenomenon in which individuals within a group tend to conform to a dominant viewpoint or opinion, which can result in suboptimal decision-making. The suppression of dissenting opinions, reduction in critical thinking, and limited exploration of alternative perspectives may occur as a means of preserving harmony and preventing conflicts.

The phenomenon of domination by a select few members is observed in certain group settings, where a small number of individuals wield a disproportionate amount of

[11] Osborn, A. F. (1953). Applied Imagination: Principles and Procedures of Creative Problem Solving. Charles Scribner's Sons.

influence over the decision-making process. The aforementioned phenomenon may lead to the marginalization of viewpoints held by other members of the group, ultimately resulting in decision outcomes that are less inclusive and balanced.

In the context of group decision making, it is common to seek a mutually agreeable solution or a compromise that meets the preferences of multiple stakeholders, even if it falls short of an optimal outcome. Consequently, the ultimate determination may not invariably represent the most advantageous resolution, but instead a compromise that may not entirely redress the fundamental issue.

Group decision-making processes may result in conflicts and disagreements among participants. Divergent viewpoints, varying interests, and discrepant priorities may engender protracted discussions or interpersonal discord, thereby impeding the advancement of the decision-making procedure and impacting the collective interactions among group members.

It is imperative to take into account the benefits and drawbacks associated with group decision making when contemplating this approach. Efficiently handling group dynamics, promoting transparent communication, cultivating a cooperative atmosphere, and employing systematic decision-making methodologies can optimize the benefits of group decision-making while mitigating its drawbacks.

6.2 Techniques for Group Decision Making

The process of group decision making entails the active involvement of numerous individuals in a collaborative effort to arrive at a decision. Various techniques and methods can be utilized to promote efficient group decision-making. The following are frequently employed methods for making decisions in a group setting:

Brainstorming is a collaborative technique that fosters the generation of a substantial quantity of ideas or solutions in an unstructured and non-critical setting. The act of expressing one's thoughts without criticism fosters creativity and divergent thinking among participants. Following the ideation phase, the collective group can engage in a process of evaluation and refinement of the generated concepts.

The Nominal Group Technique (NGT)[12] is a systematic approach that guarantees equitable engagement and contribution from all members of a group. The methodology entails a systematic approach wherein individuals generate ideas independently, subsequently sharing them with the group, and engaging in a collaborative discussion and evaluation of the ideas. The utilization of Nominal Group Technique (NGT) serves as a means to mitigate the potential for a select few individuals to dominate group discussions and instead fosters a culture of active participation from all members.

The Delphi Method is a consensus-seeking technique utilized by a group of experts. The process entails several iterations of anonymous feedback. During each iteration, the individuals provide their responses to a set of inquiries or assertions, and the condensed feedback is subsequently disseminated among the collective. The aforementioned procedure persists until a unanimous agreement is attained or until a predetermined cessation juncture is encountered.

Multi-voting is a method employed to prioritize various options or ideas. Individuals within a given group are allocated a finite quantity of votes, such as adhesive labels or points, which they may apportion among the various options. The options that receive the greatest number of votes are regarded as the most favored. The utilization of multi-voting facilitates the process of reducing options and determining the most preferred alternatives.

The process of decision matrix analysis entails the creation of a matrix that enumerates the pertinent criteria or factors that are germane to the decision and the feasible alternatives. The process involves individual assessment or ranking of each alternative by group members based on the established criteria, and the resulting scores are

[12] Tjosvold, D., & Johnson, D. W. (2017). Conflict and Cooperation: Intragroup and Intergroup Perspectives. Routledge.

combined to yield a comprehensive evaluation. The utilization of a matrix facilitates the visualization and comparison of various alternatives, while taking into account multiple criteria in a simultaneous manner.

The SWOT analysis is a method utilized for assessing the potential advantages, limitations, prospects, and challenges linked to a particular determination or plan of action. The group collaboratively identifies and evaluates the internal strengths and weaknesses, along with the external opportunities and threats. The utilization of SWOT analysis facilitates the evaluation of the various factors that impact a decision and furnishes a comprehensive comprehension of the situation.

Consensus building is a process that entails striving towards a mutually agreed-upon resolution or verdict that is deemed satisfactory by all members of a group. Effective collaboration necessitates transparent communication, attentive listening, and a readiness to acknowledge and integrate a range of viewpoints. Consensus can be attained through the utilization of various methods, including facilitated discussions, negotiation, and compromise.

Group Decision Support Systems (GDSS) are computer-based tools and software designed to aid in group decision making processes. Group Decision Support System (GDSS) tools offer a platform for members of a group to engage in collaborative efforts, exchange information, and partake in decision-making endeavors. Frequently, these platforms incorporate functionalities such as voting, ideation, and prioritization, which augment intercommunication and information dissemination among the collective.

The implementation of these techniques necessitates the establishment of unambiguous goals, the facilitation of engaged involvement, the advocacy of transparent communication, and the proficient management of collective interactions. The selection of an appropriate methodology is contingent upon various factors, including but not limited to the intricacy of the decision, the magnitude of the group, the resources at hand, and the predilections of the members comprising the group.

6.3 Role of Leadership in Group Decision Making

Effective group decision-making is greatly aided by strong leadership. An adept leader possesses the ability to direct and sway the decision-making process, guaranteeing that the collective functions harmoniously and attains the most favorable results. The following are essential leadership functions in the context of group decision-making:

The process of group decision-making is initiated by the leader who sets the overarching vision, goals, and objectives. The provision of lucidity and guidance is essential in ensuring that the collective comprehends the intention of the resolution and the intended consequences. Establishing a distinct vision facilitates the coordination of collective endeavors and maintains concentration on the current objective.

The establishment of a supportive environment is a crucial aspect of leadership. A leader must foster an inclusive atmosphere that encourages group members to freely express their opinions and ideas without hesitation. They cultivate a milieu characterized by trust, respect, and transparent communication. Leaders can foster creativity, collaboration, and constructive debate within a group by promoting active participation and acknowledging diverse perspectives.

Leadership's Facilitative Role in Decision-Making: Leaders are responsible for guiding the decision-making process through facilitation. The individuals in charge guarantee that the collective adheres to a methodical methodology, complies with predetermined schedules, and takes into account all pertinent data and perspectives. Leadership involves the facilitation of discussions, promotion of active listening, and management of conflicts or disagreements that may arise. In addition, they facilitate the process of consensus-building and assist the group in arriving at a collective decision.

Leaders frequently contribute their specialized knowledge and expertise to inform the decision-making process. The individuals provide pertinent information, data, and perspectives that aid in informing the collective deliberations and examination. Leaders impart their knowledge to facilitate the group's comprehension of the situation, deliberate on multiple options, and assess the possible advantages or disadvantages linked with the resolution.

The effective management of group dynamics is an essential aspect of leadership, which involves ensuring equitable participation of all members. Effective leaders promote equitable opportunities for all members of a group to make contributions, thereby mitigating the potential for a small subset of individuals to dominate the group. The aforementioned practices foster active participation, facilitate equitable decision-making, and address potential conflicts or disparities in power dynamics that may emerge among group members.

Leaders foster critical thinking and evaluation skills in group members by utilizing techniques such as posing thought-provoking inquiries, questioning assumptions, and promoting comprehensive examination of alternative solutions. The organization fosters a culture that prioritizes evidence-based decision making, wherein decisions are substantiated by rational thought, empirical data, and logical inference. Leadership involves the responsibility of facilitating the group's assessment of the potential outcomes and trade-offs that are linked to each available option.

In certain circumstances where a timely resolution is necessary or when consensus cannot be achieved, leaders may possess the responsibility and authority to make the ultimate decision. Effective leaders take into account the viewpoints, insights, and proposals of their team members, while also factoring in the wider organizational or strategic implications before arriving at a conclusive determination.

The act of communicating and implementing decisions is a critical responsibility of leaders, as they are tasked with disseminating the decision to the group and pertinent stakeholders. The authors furnish lucid explications, justifications, and directives pertaining to the execution of the resolution. Efficient communication plays a crucial role in ensuring that all stakeholders comprehend and approve the decision, thereby promoting seamless execution and implementation.

The act of leadership in the context of group decision making does not involve the imposition of one's own ideas or the exertion of control over the group. The task at hand involves the facilitation of collaboration, guidance of the process, and utilization of the collective wisdom and expertise of the group to arrive at the most favorable decisions. An adept leader establishes a setting that enables the team, amplifies their capacity to make decisions, and cultivates a feeling of possession and dedication to the results.

6.4 Handling Conflicts in Group Decision Making

Robust leadership significantly facilitates efficient group decision-making. A proficient leader exhibits the capacity to guide and influence the process of decision-making, ensuring that the group operates cohesively and achieves optimal outcomes. The subsequent functions are imperative in leadership within the framework of group decision-making:

The leader is responsible for initiating the group decision-making process by establishing the overarching vision, goals, and objectives. Clarity and direction are crucial in facilitating a shared understanding of the purpose of the resolution and its anticipated outcomes. The act of formulating a clear and unique perspective enables the synchronization of group undertakings and sustains focus on the present goal.

Creating a conducive atmosphere is an essential element of effective leadership. It is imperative for a leader to cultivate an all-encompassing environment that promotes the uninhibited expression of viewpoints and concepts by group constituents. The individuals in question foster an environment that is distinguished by the presence of trust, respect, and open communication. Effective leadership can facilitate the cultivation of innovative thinking, cooperative teamwork, and productive discourse among team members through the encouragement of active engagement and recognition of varying viewpoints.

The facilitative role of leadership in decision-making entails the responsibility of leaders to guide and oversee the decision-making process. The responsible authorities ensure that the group follows a systematic approach, adheres to pre-established timelines, and considers all relevant information and viewpoints. Leadership encompasses the facilitation of dialogues, advocacy of attentive listening, and resolution of conflicts or divergences that may emerge. Furthermore, they aid in the facilitation of consensus-building and support the group in reaching a unified decision.

Leaders often provide their domain-specific knowledge and expertise to facilitate the process of making informed decisions. The individuals contribute relevant information, data, and perspectives that assist in informing the group's collective deliberations and analysis. Leaders communicate their expertise to aid the collective understanding of the circumstances, engage in a process of considering various alternatives, and evaluate the potential benefits or drawbacks associated with the decision.

The proficient administration of group dynamics constitutes a crucial facet of leadership, encompassing the maintenance of fair and impartial involvement of all members. Leaders who are effective ensure that every member of a group has equal opportunities to contribute, which helps prevent a small group of individuals from dominating the group. The practices mentioned above promote engagement, enable fair decision-making, and tackle possible conflicts or imbalances in power dynamics that could arise among members of a group.

Leaders facilitate the development of critical thinking and evaluation abilities among group members through the implementation of strategies such as presenting thought-provoking queries, challenging assumptions, and encouraging thorough exploration of alternative solutions. The organization cultivates a culture that places emphasis on making decisions based on evidence, whereby decisions are supported by logical reasoning, empirical evidence, and deductive reasoning. The act of leadership entails the duty of enabling the group to evaluate the possible consequences and compromises associated with every viable alternative.

In specific situations where prompt resolution is imperative or when agreement cannot be reached, leaders may bear the obligation and power to render the final verdict. Competent leaders consider the perspectives, ideas, and suggestions of their subordinates, while also taking into consideration the broader organizational or strategic ramifications before making a definitive decision.

The dissemination and implementation of decisions is a crucial responsibility of leaders, who are charged with communicating the decision to the group and relevant stakeholders. The authors provide clear explanations, justifications, and instructions regarding the implementation of the resolution. Effective communication is essential in ensuring that all parties involved understand and endorse the decision, which facilitates smooth execution and implementation.

In the context of group decision making, leadership does not entail the imposition of personal ideas or exertion of control over the group. The objective of this undertaking entails the promotion of cooperation, direction of the procedure, and application of the combined knowledge and proficiency of the team to attain the most advantageous resolutions. A proficient leader creates an environment that facilitates the team, enhances their decision-making abilities, and fosters a sense of ownership and commitment towards the outcomes.

Chapter 7: Ethical Considerations in Decision Making

In this chapter, we delve into the role of ethics in decision making. Ethical considerations can greatly impact the decision-making process and its outcomes, highlighting the importance of making decisions that are not just profitable, but also morally sound and socially responsible.

7.1 What is Ethical Decision Making?

The concept of ethical decision making pertains to the systematic assessment and selection of conduct or deeds that are consistent with moral precepts, principles, and ethical benchmarks. The process entails the examination of ethical ramifications and possible outcomes of choices, in addition to the entitlements, welfare, and concerns of persons and impacted parties. The process of making ethical decisions is informed by fundamental values such as impartiality, uprightness, veracity, deference, and communal accountability. The objective is to select options that align with moral principles and ethical standards. The following are fundamental components of ethical decision-making:

The process of ethical decision making is initiated by the identification and acknowledgement of ethical dilemmas and issues, thereby demonstrating ethical awareness. The process entails the identification of scenarios that encompass conflicting values, potential harm, or ethical considerations. Individuals must possess sensitivity towards the ethical implications of their actions and the potential impact on others in order to demonstrate ethical awareness.

The process of ethical decision-making is informed by ethical standards and principles that serve as a structure for assessing options. The origins of these standards may be diverse, encompassing professional codes of conduct, organizational values, legal mandates, societal conventions, or individual convictions. Ethical standards offer a framework of principles and values that serve as a reference point for assessing and appraising decisions and behaviors.

The process of ethical decision making entails a methodical examination and assessment of the ethical aspects inherent in a given scenario. The process entails a careful evaluation of the possible outcomes, advantages, and drawbacks associated with various courses of action. The process of ethical analysis involves the evaluation of various factors such as the protection of individual rights and welfare, equitable treatment, impartiality, and the wider societal implications of choices.

The process of ethical decision making necessitates the application of deliberate and analytical reasoning. The process necessitates individuals to engage in introspection regarding the ethical principles, values, and moral reasoning that underlie their decision-making. The process of ethical reasoning involves the examination of ethical theories and frameworks that can provide guidance for decision-making. These may include consequentialism, deontology, virtue ethics, or ethical relativism.

The process of ethical decision-making involves the consideration of the interests and concerns of diverse stakeholders who may be impacted by the decision. The process entails taking into account the viewpoints and entitlements of individuals or collectives who possess a vested interest in the result. Ethical decision-makers strive to achieve equilibrium among the interests of diverse stakeholders and render decisions that advance the common good while mitigating harm.

The ethical process of decision making necessitates the presence of transparency and accountability. Transparency is a crucial aspect of decision-making, which entails candidly disclosing the decision-making process, the variables taken into account, and the rationale underpinning the selected course of action. Individuals who make ethical decisions demonstrate accountability for their actions and are prepared to provide rationale and clarification for their choices.

The concept of Continuous Ethical Improvement posits that ethical decision making is a perpetual process of acquiring knowledge and enhancing one's ethical reasoning abilities. The process entails a perpetual introspection of prior choices, soliciting input, and modifying moral principles in accordance with acquired knowledge. Individuals who are responsible for making ethical decisions endeavor to improve their ethical acuity, expertise, and competencies in order to make progressively well-informed and ethical decisions.

The practice of ethical decision-making is a crucial component in a multitude of settings, encompassing personal affairs, commercial enterprises, healthcare provision, legal proceedings, and governmental policymaking. The promotion of integrity, fairness, and social responsibility is believed to make a significant contribution towards the establishment of a more just and ethical society. The process of ethical decision making is aimed at ensuring that both individuals and organizations align their actions with their values and moral principles, while taking into account the wider implications of their decisions on the community and individuals.

7.2 The Importance of Ethical Decision Making

The significance of ethical decision making is paramount in both personal and professional domains. The significance of ethical decision making can be attributed to several factors.

The maintenance of personal and professional integrity is contingent upon the practice of ethical decision making, which is of paramount importance. The consistent display of ethical decision-making by individuals is indicative of their unwavering dedication to upholding principles of honesty, fairness, and ethical conduct. The cultivation of trust and credibility is conducive to fostering positive relationships, be it at the individual level or within organizational settings.

The maintenance of a positive reputation and legitimacy is facilitated by ethical decision-making. Entities and persons recognized for their adherence to ethical principles are inclined to garner confidence, admiration, and backing from their stakeholders. The practice of ethical decision making plays a pivotal role in cultivating a reputation of dependability, which is deemed indispensable for attaining sustained prosperity.

The promotion of fairness and justice is facilitated through ethical decision making, which guarantees the upholding of these values. Ethical decision-making endeavors to attain fair outcomes by taking into account the rights and interests of all stakeholders involved. Making ethical decisions involves refraining from discriminatory practices, biases, and favoritism, thereby fostering a perception of impartiality in both personal and professional interactions.

Improving the Quality of Decision-Making: The incorporation of ethical considerations in decision-making processes has been shown to result in superior quality decisions[13]. The act of contemplating ethical implications facilitates critical thinking, enables individuals to evaluate various options, and encourages them to reflect on the enduring outcomes of their decisions. Moral principles, values, and ethical standards are considered by ethical decision makers, leading to more deliberate and sound decision-making.

The ethical decision-making process aims to reduce harm and enhance benefits for both individuals and society. In ethical decision-making, due consideration is given to the potential ramifications for various stakeholders, such as employees, customers, communities, and the environment. Ethical decision makers strive to generate favorable consequences and prevent unwarranted harm by considering the welfare of others.

[13] Velasquez, M. (2012). Business Ethics: Concepts and Cases. Pearson.

The adherence to ethical principles in decision making processes guarantees conformity with legal and regulatory frameworks. The concept of ethical conduct extends beyond mere adherence to legal norms, as it encompasses moral and ethical responsibilities that may not be explicitly delineated by legal mandates. The act of making ethical decisions serves as a means for individuals and organizations to reduce the likelihood of legal transgressions and the resultant repercussions.

The cultivation of a positive organizational culture can be facilitated by ethical decision-making practices. The cultivation and implementation of ethical conduct throughout all tiers of an enterprise establishes a precedent for a workplace culture that is characterized by ethical, inclusive, and respectful practices. The implementation of ethical decision-making processes fosters a culture of teamwork, trust, and collaboration, which in turn leads to improved employee morale and enhanced organizational performance.

The alignment of ethical decision making with social responsibility and sustainable development is a crucial aspect to consider. Ethical decision-making involves taking into account the wider implications for society, the natural world, and future cohorts. Through the practice of ethical behavior, both individuals and organizations can make a positive impact on society and strive towards a more sustainable and equitable global community.

The process of ethical decision making is conducive to fostering personal growth and development. The proccss of ethical decision-making necessitates introspection, analytical reasoning, and ethical deliberation. Through deliberate participation in ethical decision-making, individuals can fortify their ethical framework, augment their capacity to make sound judgments, and cultivate a more profound comprehension of their values and principles.

The importance of ethical decision-making cannot be overstated in the context of ethical leadership. Leaders who consistently demonstrate ethical decision-making serve as a role model for their subordinates and foster ethical conduct within their teams and organizations. The implementation of ethical leadership fosters an environment that upholds principles of honesty, answerability, and ethical obligation.

To summarize, the process of making ethical decisions is of utmost importance for upholding personal and professional integrity, promoting fairness and trust, and contributing to a positive impact on society. Through the consideration of ethical implications, both individuals and organizations can make informed and responsible decisions that align with moral principles, thereby contributing to their own success and the advancement of society at large.

7.3 Framework for Ethical Decision Making

The facilitation of ethical decision making can be achieved through adherence to a framework that offers a methodical approach to assessing and selecting ethical options. The following is a frequently employed framework for ethical decision-making:

Commence by precisely recognizing the ethical predicament or quandary currently under consideration. Comprehend the divergent principles, concerns, or ethical deliberations entailed in the determination[14]. Assess the possible ramifications and identify the parties that could be impacted by the resolution.

Acquire Pertinent Data: Compile all pertinent information, facts, and data pertaining to the ethical matter. It is imperative to possess a thorough comprehension of the circumstances at hand, encompassing any relevant legal statutes, regulatory frameworks, or institutional guidelines. It is advisable to adopt a multifaceted approach by considering diverse viewpoints and soliciting input from individuals who possess specialized knowledge or unique insights pertaining to the subject matter.

Determine Ethical Principles and Standards: Determine the ethical principles, values, and standards that pertain to the decision at hand. It is advisable to contemplate ethical

[14] Treviño, L. K., & Nelson, K. A. (2016). Managing Business Ethics: Straight Talk about How to Do It Right. Wiley.

frameworks, such as consequentialism, deontology, virtue ethics, or ethical relativism, in order to make informed ethical decisions. Identify the ethical principles that ought to inform your decision-making procedure.

Conduct an assessment of alternative courses of action to effectively tackle the ethical issue at hand. Evaluate the potential ramifications, advantages, and hazards linked with every alternative. It is important to evaluate how each option corresponds with the ethical principles and values that have been identified. Conduct a critical analysis of the rights, well-being, and interests of the various stakeholders who are implicated in the matter at hand.

Formulate a decision and provide a rationale for it, drawing on the assessment of available options, that you deem to be the most ethical and morally defensible. Please provide a clear and well-supported rationale for your decision, elucidating how it conforms to the ethical principles and values that you have identified. It is important to evaluate how the decision contributes to the principles of equity, impartiality, and the general welfare of those involved.

Execute the Decision: Formulate a comprehensive strategy to efficiently execute the decision. It is imperative to contemplate the pragmatic measures, necessary resources, and temporal parameters that are requisite to implement the decision. It is imperative to effectively communicate the decision to all pertinent stakeholders and ensure their comprehension of the underlying reasoning.

Upon executing the decision, it is imperative to engage in a process of reflection and learning. This involves a critical examination of the outcomes and ethical implications of the chosen course of action. Evaluate whether the decision has successfully attained the intended ethical objectives and determine if any modifications or enhancements are necessary. Engaging in introspection regarding the process of decision-making facilitates ongoing education and development in the realm of ethical decision-making.

It is noteworthy that the aforementioned framework offers a methodical methodology, notwithstanding that ethical decision making may remain intricate and arduous. Ethical predicaments may necessitate the weighing of alternatives and the making of arduous decisions. It is advisable to consult with reliable mentors, ethics committees, or professional associations when confronted with intricate ethical dilemmas.

It is imperative to acknowledge that ethical decision making is a perpetual procedure that necessitates persistent contemplation, education, and introspection. Individuals can improve their decision-making abilities and promote a more ethical and responsible society by adhering to a structured framework and upholding ethical principles.

7.4 Ethical Theories in Decision Making

Ethical theories offer a set of principles and frameworks that aid in ethical decision-making by presenting varying viewpoints on the determination of moral rightness or wrongness. The following are notable ethical theories that are frequently utilized in the process of decision-making:

Utilitarianism is an ethical theory that falls under the consequentialist category, which prioritizes the outcome of an action over the action itself. The central tenet of this theory is to maximize the overall happiness or utility. Utilitarianism posits that the ethical course of action is that which yields the highest degree of happiness or utility for the largest possible group of individuals. Utilitarianism is a decision-making approach that entails assessing the potential outcomes of various alternatives and selecting the one that maximizes the collective welfare.

Deontology is a philosophical approach that places emphasis on moral duty and the adherence to rules and principles. It is often associated with the renowned philosopher Immanuel Kant. Deontological ethics is a moral framework that posits the existence of actions or principles that are intrinsically right or wrong, irrespective of their outcomes. Deontology is a moral framework that prioritizes adherence to ethical principles, such as honesty, fairness, and respect for autonomy, in decision-making processes. This approach emphasizes the importance of upholding these principles, rather than solely focusing on the outcomes of decisions.

Virtue Ethics is a philosophical approach that centers on the cultivation of virtuous character traits and underscores the significance of moral virtues in the process of making ethical decisions. The proposition posits that the manifestation of ethical conduct is a result of the development and nurturing of virtuous attributes, such as veracity, empathy, uprightness, and fortitude. Virtue ethics is a decision-making approach that involves evaluating how various choices align with virtuous qualities and striving to undertake actions that foster moral excellence.

Ethical relativism is a philosophical stance that asserts that ethical principles and judgments are contingent upon the perspectives of individuals, cultures, or societies. The proposition posits that moral values and principles are subject to contextual variations, and that there are no absolute or universally applicable moral truths. Ethical relativism acknowledges that ethical decisions are influenced by cultural norms, personal beliefs, and situational factors in the process of decision-making.

Rights-based ethics is a moral framework that centers on the fundamental rights and inherent dignity of individuals. The statement underscores the notion that there exist certain inherent entitlements that are vested in individuals, which warrant due consideration and safeguarding. Rights-based ethics is a decision-making approach that involves taking into account the rights of all stakeholders and ensuring that decisions made do not contravene or encroach upon those rights.

Care ethics is a philosophical approach that places great importance on the role of relationships, empathy, and care in the process of making ethical decisions. The proposition posits that decision-making processes ought to accord precedence to the welfare of others, fostering social connections, and acknowledging the interdependence among individuals. The ethical framework of care holds particular pertinence in decision-making processes that encompass considerations of interpersonal relationships, empathetic understanding, and the welfare of others.

Ethical egoism is a philosophical perspective that advocates for individuals to prioritize their own self-interest, with the aim of pursuing their own happiness and well-being. The statement posits that individuals bear a moral responsibility to prioritize their personal interests over those of others. The ethical theory of egoism in decision making entails evaluating the possible advantages and disadvantages to oneself and selecting options that optimize self-interest.

It is noteworthy that these ethical theories may offer divergent viewpoints on ethical decision-making and may occasionally present incongruities with one another. In practical scenarios, individuals and organizations may resort to a variety of ethical theories or amalgamate principles from diverse theories to steer their decision-making processes, contingent upon the particular circumstances and the values they accord precedence. The process of ethical decision making necessitates a deliberate and reflective approach, involving the utilization of analytical reasoning and ethical frameworks that are consistent with an individual's personal beliefs and the intended ethical consequences.

Chapter 8: Evaluating and Learning from Past Decisions

This chapter highlights the final step in the decision-making process: reviewing and learning from past decisions. It is a crucial part of the process, often overlooked but vital to improving future decision-making.

8.1 Importance of Decision Evaluation

The process of decision evaluation is a critical component of the decision-making process, which entails the appraisal of the decision's outcomes and efficacy. The process of comprehending the consequences of one's choices and actions, reflecting on the acquired knowledge, and implementing enhancements for subsequent decision-making is beneficial for both individuals and entities. The significance of decision evaluation can be underscored by several key reasons.

The process of decision evaluation enables individuals to gauge the efficacy or success of a decision. This affords the chance to juxtapose the intended goals and aims of the determination with the factual outcomes attained. Through the process of assessing the efficacy of a given decision, individuals can discern the domains in which it has proven successful, as well as those that may necessitate modifications or enhancements.

The process of decision evaluation facilitates the identification and subsequent learning from mistakes or errors in judgment. The decision's potential shortcomings, flaws, or unintended consequences can be illuminated through the insights provided. Through the process of analyzing errors, individuals can acquire valuable insights that can enhance their future decision-making abilities and improve the overall quality of their decisions.

The process of decision evaluation enables individuals and organizations to discern best practices and lessons learned from successful decision-making. Through comprehension of successful outcomes, individuals can discern optimal methodologies and approaches that can be implemented in forthcoming scenarios involving decision-making. The process of evaluating decisions facilitates the acquisition and dissemination of knowledge and insights that can be leveraged to augment decision-making proficiency.

The practice of decision evaluation fosters accountability and transparency in the process of decision making. The statement exemplifies a dedication to acquiring knowledge from the results of choices made and assuming accountability for the resultant effects. Through transparently assessing their choices, both individuals and institutions can exhibit their readiness to contemplate their behaviors and implement requisite modifications.

The practice of evaluating decisions fosters a culture of ongoing enhancement. The practice of encouraging individuals and organizations to engage in introspection regarding their decision-making processes, evaluate their areas of proficiency and deficiency, and recognize prospects for enhancement is advocated. Through regular assessment of their choices, individuals can improve their decision-making proficiency and augment their capacity to make well-informed and efficacious decisions.

The process of decision evaluation facilitates adaptability and flexibility for individuals and organizations in their decision-making methodologies. The process aids in the identification of evolving circumstances, emerging patterns, and novel data that may necessitate modifications to prior decisions. The assessment of decisions facilitates adaptability and the capacity to react to changing circumstances.

The process of decision evaluation presents a favorable occasion for stakeholders to engage and offer their input regarding the consequences of decisions. The involvement of stakeholders in the evaluation process enables the collection of diverse perspectives, comprehension of the decision's impact on different stakeholders, and the establishment of more robust relationships founded on transparency and accountability for individuals and organizations.

The process of decision evaluation aids in the assessment of the congruence between decisions made and the strategic goals and objectives of an organization. This facilitates the assessment of the alignment of decisions with the mission, vision, and long-term plans of both individuals and organizations[15]. The process of decision evaluation serves to facilitate strategic decision making by verifying that the options being considered align with the overarching goals and preferences of the individual or entity in question.

Through acknowledging the significance of assessing decisions, both individuals and organizations can foster a climate of perpetual learning, enhancement, and knowledgeable decision-making. The process of assessing decisions enables the recognition of their merits, drawbacks, and potential for advancement, resulting in enhanced and triumphant decision-making consequences.

8.2 Key Aspects of Decision Evaluation

The process of decision evaluation entails the critical examination of the results and efficacy of a decision with the aim of ascertaining its triumph and pinpointing avenues for enhancement. When performing a thorough decision evaluation, it is important to take into account several critical factors.

The establishment of objectives and criteria for the decision should be clearly defined. These benchmarks function as standards by which the results and efficacy of the decision will be assessed. In order to ensure clarity in evaluation, it is imperative that the objectives and criteria are formulated in a manner that adheres to the SMART

[15] Tversky, A., & Kahneman, D. (1974). Judgment under Uncertainty: Heuristics and Biases. Science, 185(4157), 1124-1131.

framework, which entails that they are specific, measurable, achievable, relevant, and time-bound.

Evaluate the factual outcomes and results of the decision. Conduct a comparative analysis of the aforementioned entities in relation to the predetermined objectives and criteria. Conduct an analysis of both quantitative and qualitative data to ascertain whether the decision has successfully attained its intended outcomes. It is important to evaluate the potential effects of a decision in both the immediate future and the distant future, while also recognizing any unforeseen outcomes that may arise.

The process of data collection and analysis involves the acquisition of pertinent data and information for the purpose of assessing a decision. This may encompass a range of pertinent indicators such as financial data, performance metrics, customer feedback, market data, or other relevant metrics. Utilize suitable statistical methodologies, qualitative analysis approaches, and comparative evaluations to derive insights regarding the outcomes of the decision.

It is recommended to solicit input from stakeholders who have been impacted by or participated in the decision-making process. Gather the viewpoints, beliefs, and personal encounters pertaining to the consequences of the decision. It is imperative to take into account the perspectives of both internal stakeholders, such as employees and managers, and external stakeholders, such as customers, suppliers, and community members. The feedback from stakeholders offers significant insights and a comprehensive perspective on the ramifications of the decision.

Key Takeaways: Determine the fundamental insights acquired from the process of making decisions and the resulting consequences. Evaluate the strengths and weaknesses of the approach taken and identify areas for potential enhancement. Critically evaluate any errors, obstacles, or accomplishments experienced throughout the process of making a decision. It is recommended to record these acquired insights to enhance the quality of decision-making processes in the future.

In the context of decision-making, it is recommended to conduct comparisons and benchmarks to evaluate the outcomes. This involves comparing the decision outcomes with relevant benchmarks or industry standards, if applicable. The aforementioned approach enables a contextual evaluation of the efficacy of the decision and furnishes valuable perspectives on the decision's performance in comparison to analogous scenarios or optimal methodologies. Comparisons and benchmarks have the potential to identify both strengths and weaknesses in a given context.

Undertake a cost-benefit analysis to evaluate the monetary and non-monetary consequences of the decision. Assess the expenses accrued and the advantages obtained as a result of the determination. It is important to take into account both quantifiable and non-quantifiable costs and benefits. This analysis facilitates the evaluation of the comprehensive worth and ROI of the decision.

The ethical considerations must be assessed in order to evaluate the potential implications of the decision. Evaluate whether the decision was in compliance with ethical principles, values, and standards. Evaluate the presence of ethical quandaries and the measures taken to resolve them. Contemplate the ethical implications of the decision and its effects on the rights, welfare, and equity of stakeholders.

Continuous improvement involves the identification of areas that require enhancement based on the findings of the evaluation. Utilize the knowledge acquired through the assessment to enhance the procedures, tactics, and methodologies involved in making decisions. Execute remedial measures, effectuate essential modifications, and assimilate the acquired knowledge into forthcoming decision-making methodologies.

The process of evaluation, along with its findings and recommendations, should be duly documented and reported. Produce a thorough document that outlines the findings and observations gathered from the assessment. It is imperative to convey the results and suggestions to pertinent stakeholders, guaranteeing openness and responsibility in the process of making decisions.

Through the careful consideration of these fundamental elements of decision evaluation, both individuals and organizations can acquire valuable insights, implement informed enhancements, and augment their decision-making proficiencies. The process of evaluating decisions promotes a culture of learning, adaptability, and ongoing improvement, ultimately leading to more efficient and prosperous decision-making results in the long run.

8.3 Learning from Past Decisions

Learning from past choices is crucial for both personal and professional development because it enables people and organizations to reflect on their experiences, understand what worked well, and pinpoint areas for improvement. The following are essential factors to contemplate when deriving insights from previous decisions:

This prompt invites reflection on the decision-making process that was employed during a particular phase. Evaluate the methodology employed in making the decision, the data and assets that were taken into account, and the engagement of relevant parties. Assess the efficacy of the decision-making procedure, including the utilization of communication, cooperation, and troubleshooting methodologies.

Conduct an assessment of the outcomes and results of the decision made. Assess the degree to which the intended goals were accomplished. Conduct an analysis of both the favorable and unfavorable results, along with any inadvertent effects. Assess the efficacy of the decision by analyzing its immediate and enduring effects.

The task at hand is to identify the pivotal factors that had an impact on the decision-making process and its subsequent outcomes. The aforementioned factors encompass both internal and external elements, namely data, market conditions, timing, resources, and stakeholder dynamics. Comprehend the influence of these variables on the decision and its consequences, and evaluate whether they were sufficiently taken into account during the decision-making procedure.

Conduct an analysis of achievements and errors by identifying the favorable outcomes and advantageous elements of the decision. Comprehend the factors that led to successful results and identify the elements that positively influenced such outcomes. Likewise, examine the errors or difficulties that were faced. Identify the fundamental underlying factors that led to these errors and contemplate potential measures that could have been implemented to avert or alleviate them.

Solicit Feedback: Request input from pertinent stakeholders who were either implicated or impacted by the determination. Collect the viewpoints and analyses of individuals regarding the decision and its resultant effects. The provision of feedback from diverse viewpoints can yield significant insights and pinpoint areas for enhancement. It is advisable to take into account input from both internal stakeholders, such as team members and colleagues, as well as external stakeholders, including customers, clients, and partners.

Determine Key Takeaways: Ascertain the key takeaways derived from the process of decision-making and its resultant outcomes. It is recommended to engage in reflection regarding one's experiences and insights, and to document them for future reference. It is imperative to take into account the knowledge, skills, and optimal methodologies that were attained or recognized during the course of the decision-making procedure.

Incorporate Enhancements: Drawing from the acquired knowledge, pinpoint domains that require enhancement and formulate strategies to execute essential modifications. One should contemplate on how the knowledge acquired from prior decisions can contribute to and improve forthcoming decision-making procedures. Execute enhancements to decision-making models, channels of communication, techniques for data analysis, or methods for engaging stakeholders.

Facilitate Knowledge Sharing and Dissemination: Foster the dissemination of best practices and lessons learned among peers. Articulate the experiential knowledge, perspectives, and suggestions that have emerged as a consequence of prior decision-making. The act of disseminating knowledge can yield advantages for coworkers, groups, or the overall institution by circumventing comparable errors, advocating for superior decision-making methodologies, and cultivating an environment of ongoing education.

Utilize and Implement Knowledge: Utilize the knowledge acquired from previous decisions to make informed decisions in future scenarios. Utilize the acquired knowledge to provide insight and direction for subsequent decisions. Modify decision-making methodologies, tactics, and procedures in accordance with the insights and enhancements discerned from past decisions.

It is recommended to integrate routine reviews and reflections into the decision-making process. It is recommended to engage in periodic evaluations of past decisions and their outcomes in order to facilitate continuous learning and improvement. It is advisable to consistently explore prospects for enhancing decision-making processes in light of the changing requirements and encounters of the individuals or entity involved.

Through the process of actively reflecting on past decisions, both individuals and organizations can leverage their experiences, circumvent the repetition of errors, and consistently enhance their capacity for effective decision-making. Studying historical events promotes a mindset of progress, flexibility, and well-informed judgment.

8.4 Role of Feedback in Learning

The provision of feedback is a pivotal aspect of the learning process, as it furnishes individuals and organizations with significant information and perspectives that facilitate enhancement and expansion. The following are significant elements that underscore the significance of feedback in the process of learning:

The process of receiving feedback assists individuals in recognizing their strengths and areas that require improvement. This offers an extrinsic viewpoint regarding an individual's aptitude, expertise, proficiencies, or conduct. Individuals can enhance their performance by identifying and capitalizing on their strengths, while constructive feedback on areas requiring improvement can assist them in directing their learning endeavors and implementing necessary modifications.

The act of enhancing self-awareness can be facilitated through feedback mechanisms, as it affords individuals with valuable insights into their blind spots, biases, or areas that may have previously eluded their attention. This facilitates individuals' comprehension of the ways in which their actions and behaviors influence both others and the ultimate results. The cultivation of self-awareness is a pivotal component of both personal and professional development, as it facilitates a deeper comprehension of one's own character and influence on others.

The provision of feedback serves as a catalyst for promoting reflective practices and critical thinking among individuals, as it prompts them to engage in introspection regarding their performance, decisions, or actions. The act of stimulating critical thinking is achieved through the promotion of self-analysis, wherein individuals are encouraged to evaluate their personal strengths, weaknesses, and opportunities for growth. By engaging in introspection and analytical reasoning, individuals can attain more profound understandings, question their presuppositions, and produce novel viewpoints, resulting in improved educational outcomes.

Feedback serves as a source of motivation and encouragement for individuals to persist in their pursuit of knowledge and skill development. Positive feedback is a valuable tool that recognizes and strengthens an individual's positive attributes and accomplishments, thereby enhancing their self-assurance and overall well-being. Providing constructive feedback in a supportive manner can aid individuals in identifying areas for improvement and motivate them to pursue growth and development.

Enabling the Process of Ongoing Enhancement: The provision of feedback is a crucial component for the achievement of continuous improvement. This facilitates individuals to track their advancement, assess the efficiency of their endeavors, and implement requisite modifications. Frequent feedback mechanisms facilitate the identification of patterns, trends, and areas of sustained growth or decline, thereby allowing individuals to optimize their learning approaches and augment their overall performance.

The receipt of feedback from diverse sources has the potential to broaden an individual's knowledge and understanding by providing varied perspectives and insights. This facilitates the exposure of individuals to diverse perspectives, concepts, and methodologies. By integrating diverse feedback perspectives, individuals can expand their cognitive horizons and adopt novel approaches to knowledge acquisition and problem resolution.

The facilitation of collaboration and communication among individuals and teams can be achieved through the provision of feedback. The aforementioned statement highlights the establishment of a conducive and encouraging atmosphere that fosters the exchange of ideas, feedback, and knowledge among individuals. The implementation of efficient feedback mechanisms fosters the practice of attentive listening, mutual regard, and positive discourse, thereby augmenting cooperation and communal acquisition of knowledge.

The provision of feedback serves to align the goals and expectations of either an individual or an organization. The mechanism in question facilitates the clarification of expectations, thereby ensuring that individuals possess a clear understanding of their obligations. Through the alignment of objectives, feedback facilitates the concentration of an individual's learning endeavors on the areas that are most pertinent to accomplishing the intended results[16].

The establishment and maintenance of trust and relationships can be facilitated through the provision of constructive and timely feedback, which serves to enhance trust and fortify relationships. When feedback is communicated in a manner that demonstrates

[16] Ariely, D. (2008). Predictably Irrational: The Hidden Forces That Shape Our Decisions. HarperCollins.

respect, empathy, and a sincere intention to facilitate development, individuals experience a sense of appreciation and comprehension. Establishing trustworthy relationships creates a conducive atmosphere wherein individuals are more receptive to receiving feedback, thereby augmenting the process of learning.

The process of decision making is facilitated by feedback, as it offers valuable insights into the consequences of actions or choices. This aids individuals in making informed decisions by comprehending how their actions or achievements impact results. The incorporation of feedback can enhance the efficacy of decision-making processes by taking into account the diverse viewpoints and personal encounters of individuals.

Through acknowledging and adopting feedback as an essential component of the educational process, both individuals and institutions can foster a climate of perpetual advancement, cooperation, and individual development. The provision of feedback is considered a crucial factor in facilitating the process of learning, as it promotes personal growth, flexibility, and the attainment of desired outcomes.

Chapter 9: Strategic Decision Making

In this final chapter, we focus on strategic decision making. While all the previous steps apply to strategic decisions, they often have a broader scope, higher stakes, and longer time horizons, demanding a more comprehensive approach.

9.1 What is Strategic Decision Making?

The term "strategic decision making" pertains to the act of making choices that bear substantial influence on the enduring trajectory, objectives, and accomplishments of an individual, entity, or enterprise. The process entails the evaluation of multiple variables, examination of possible consequences, and determination of the optimal approach to attain strategic goals. Strategic decisions generally encompass the distribution of resources, establishment of priorities, and implementation of choices that influence the overarching strategy of an organization. The following are fundamental components of strategic decision making:

Strategic decision making entails adopting a long-term perspective and evaluating the ramifications of decisions on the overall trajectory and prosperity of an individual or entity. The process entails establishing specific targets and aims that are in accordance with the organization's overarching vision and mission, and striving towards attaining a durable competitive edge.

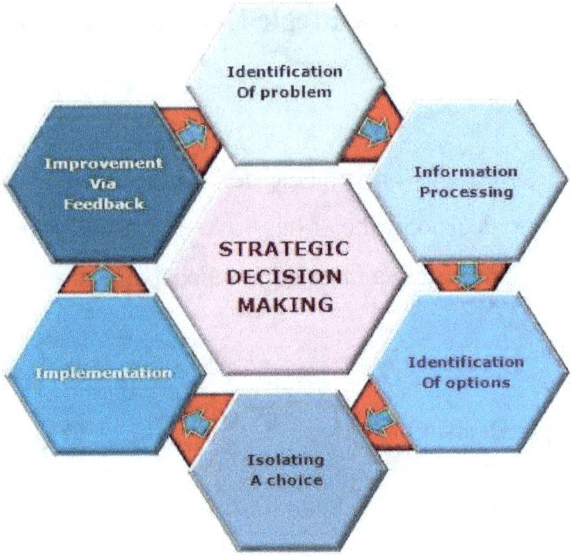

Source: Sumit K. Jha, 6 'I's Of Strategic Decision Making, Process Consultant, 2011.

The process of strategic decision making adopts a holistic approach that encompasses a broad spectrum of factors that impact the organization, including but not limited to, internal competencies, external market dynamics, competitive milieu, technological advancements, legal and regulatory framework, and socio-environmental trends. The process entails comprehending the interconnectivity among said factors and arriving at decisions that maximize the strategic alignment holistically.

Strategic decision-making processes take into account the existence of both risk and uncertainty. The process entails the evaluation of potential risks, analysis of uncertainties, and contemplation of contingency plans aimed at mitigating unfavorable outcomes. Strategic decision-making frequently entails the delicate equilibrium between risk and reward, necessitating a calculated risk-taking approach by the decision-maker to pursue strategic opportunities.

The process of making strategic decisions is heavily reliant on data and information in order to facilitate a data-driven analysis. The process entails the collection of pertinent information, carrying out an examination, and employing analytical methodologies and instruments to assess various alternatives. The utilization of data-driven analysis facilitates the evaluation of the viability, potential influence, and hazards linked to diverse strategic alternatives.

The process of strategic decision making necessitates the assessment of various alternatives and scenarios. The process entails the evaluation of various strategic alternatives, assessing their advantages and disadvantages, and ultimately choosing the optimal option that aligns with the objectives, assets, and competitive standing of the entity. Decision-makers have at their disposal a range of tools and frameworks, including SWOT analysis, cost-benefit analysis, and scenario planning, which they may employ to assess various alternatives[17].

In the context of strategic decision making, it is imperative to consider the interests and viewpoints of diverse stakeholders, such as shareholders, employees, customers, suppliers, communities, and other significant stakeholders. The process entails comprehending the requirements, anticipations, and probable consequences of the resolution on every stakeholder cohort. The process of making strategic decisions necessitates the careful consideration and balancing of the interests of various stakeholders.

Strategic decision making is a process that ensures that decisions made are in accordance with the culture, values, and ethical standards of the organization. The assessment takes into account the reputation of the organization, its brand image, and the social responsibility and ethical behavior expectations of stakeholders. It is imperative that strategic decisions align with an organization's dedication to upholding integrity and responsible business practices.

The process of strategic decision making necessitates a continuous monitoring and adaptation approach. The process entails periodic evaluation of the consequences of strategic choices, monitoring advancement towards strategic objectives, and

[17] Grant, R. M. (2003). Strategic Planning in a Turbulent Environment: Evidence from the Oil Majors. Strategic Management Journal, 24(6), 491-517.

implementing modifications when deemed appropriate. In order to effectively navigate the internal and external environment, it is imperative for strategic decision makers to possess agility and responsiveness.

The process of making strategic decisions holds significant importance for organizations as it plays a pivotal role in determining their long-term success and competitive edge. The successful execution of business operations necessitates a combination of analytical reasoning, forward-thinking planning, and adeptness in maneuvering intricate and ever-changing commercial landscapes. The ability to make strategic decisions that are effective is crucial for organizations as it enables them to anticipate and address challenges while also capitalizing on opportunities, leading to sustainable growth and improved performance.

9.2 Components of Strategic Decision Making

The process of strategic decision making encompasses various essential elements that collaboratively contribute to the creation and execution of efficacious strategies. The aforementioned components furnish a structure for evaluating the present condition, recognizing potential prospects and obstacles, and rendering judicious determinations to attain strategic goals. The principal constituents of strategic decision making are as follows:

Strategic analysis is a comprehensive evaluation of an organization's internal and external environment aimed at identifying its strengths, weaknesses, opportunities, and threats (SWOT analysis). The process entails the collection of pertinent information, execution of market investigation, assessment of competitors, examination of industry patterns, and evaluation of the organization's capacities and resources. The process of strategic analysis offers valuable insights into the present condition of an organization and facilitates the identification of domains that require strategic decision-making.

The process of strategic decision making entails establishing unambiguous and quantifiable goals and objectives that are consistent with the vision and mission of the organization. Goals offer a sense of orientation and intentionality, whereas objectives establish precise benchmarks to be attained within a predetermined time frame. Precisely defined goals and objectives serve as a navigational tool for decision-making processes, as they establish a structure for assessing strategic alternatives and efficiently distributing resources.

The process of strategic decision making involves the creation of a variety of strategic options or alternatives aimed at tackling the identified opportunities and challenges. This entails engaging in ideation, performing a thorough examination of potential scenarios, and evaluating multiple strategic methodologies. The objective is to investigate diverse approaches and cultivate numerous prospective tactics that can be assessed and contrasted.

The process of evaluating and selecting strategic options entails a comprehensive analysis of the feasibility, potential risks, expected outcomes, and resource requirements associated with each option. The process of decision-making involves a thorough analysis of the advantages and disadvantages of each available option. This analysis takes into account various factors, including but not limited to market potential, competitive advantage, financial implications, and alignment with the goals of the organization. During this phase, it is customary to employ various tools such as cost benefit analysis, risk analysis, and strategic fit analysis.

The implementation of a strategic option is a crucial aspect of strategic decision making, which entails the creation of a comprehensive plan for its execution. This encompasses the process of identifying the requisite resources, setting up schedules, delegating tasks, and specifying performance indicators and objectives. Successful execution of a chosen strategy necessitates effective implementation through the means of clear communication, coordination, and progress monitoring.

The process of strategic decision making necessitates a continuous cycle of monitoring and evaluation. The process entails monitoring the advancement of strategic initiatives, evaluating their efficacy, and contrasting factual performance with intended results. This enables decision-makers to detect variances, effectuate requisite modifications, and gain insights from the execution process.

The process of strategic decision making involves the integration of feedback loops to acquire insights and knowledge from the results of executed strategies. The provision of feedback facilitates the comprehension of decision makers regarding the consequences of their decisions, enables the identification of potential areas for enhancement, and empowers them to make informed modifications to forthcoming strategic decisions. The acquisition of knowledge from previous occurrences amplifies the capacity of an organization to adjust, create novel solutions, and formulate superior strategic judgments in the long run.

The strategic decision-making process acknowledges the importance of flexibility and adaptability in a constantly evolving business landscape. It is imperative for strategic decisions to exhibit responsiveness towards dynamic market conditions, emerging trends, and evolving customer requirements. Regularly evaluating the strategic environment, monitoring competitors, and promptly adapting strategies as necessary are essential components of effective strategic management.

Through the consideration of these components, organizations can engage in strategic decision-making that is effective, aligns with their goals, optimizes resource allocation, and enables them to navigate complex and competitive business environments. These constituents offer a methodical methodology for rendering judicious judgments and attaining enduring triumph.

9.3 Role of Risk Management in Strategic Decision Making

The process of risk management is of paramount importance in the context of strategic decision making, as it facilitates the identification, evaluation, and reduction of risks that are linked to strategic options. The process entails a methodical approach of identifying probable hazards, assessing their probability and potential consequences, and formulating tactics to handle and alleviate them. The following are essential elements that underscore the significance of risk management in the process of strategic decision-making:

The process of risk identification is a crucial aspect of risk management as it aids in the identification of potential risks that may be associated with strategic decisions. The process entails a comprehensive evaluation of both the internal and external milieu, encompassing the contemplation of diverse scenarios, and the identification of plausible uncertainties, threats, and vulnerabilities. The process of risk identification aims to provide decision makers with a comprehensive comprehension of the potential risks that may arise when pursuing specific strategic options.

Risk assessment is a process within risk management that involves evaluating the probability and potential consequences of identified risks. The process entails the measurement and assessment of potential hazards, taking into account their likelihood of transpiring and the potential impact on strategic goals. The process of risk assessment enables decision-makers to prioritize risks based on their level of significance and determine which risks necessitate greater attention and mitigation efforts.

The field of decision analysis involves the use of risk management techniques to offer decision makers valuable insights into the potential risks and rewards that are associated with various strategic options. This aids in the assessment of the trade-offs between potential advantages and associated risks. Through the incorporation of risk assessment during the decision analysis phase, decision makers are able to make informed decisions that effectively balance their risk tolerance with their desired strategic objectives.

Risk mitigation and response are integral components of risk management, which entails formulating tactics to alleviate identified risks and establish suitable courses of action. The process entails the selection of risk treatment alternatives, which may comprise of risk avoidance, risk reduction, risk transfer, or risk acceptance. Risk mitigation strategies encompass a range of measures such as the implementation of control mechanisms, diversification of strategies, development of contingency plans, or acquisition of insurance coverage. Risk management is a process that aims to provide decision makers with strategies to mitigate or address potential risks in an efficient manner.

The integration of risk management with strategic planning processes ensures the incorporation of risk considerations into the decision-making framework. The alignment of risk management activities with an organization's strategic goals and objectives is achieved. The proactive identification and mitigation of risks that may impede the attainment of strategic objectives can be facilitated by the integration of risk management and strategic planning within organizations.

The quality of strategic decision making can be improved through the implementation of risk management, which offers decision makers a methodical and organized framework for evaluating potential risks. The activity fosters the development of critical thinking skills, the ability to analyze data, and the capacity to assess alternative options in consideration of potential risks. The practice of risk management aims to provide decision makers with comprehensive knowledge of potential risks, enabling them to make informed decisions with a heightened awareness of the associated consequences.

Risk management plays a crucial role in facilitating compliance with legal and regulatory obligations, as well as fostering sound governance principles within organizations. Organizations can ensure adherence to relevant laws and regulations by taking into account the potential risks associated with strategic decisions. Risk management facilitates transparency, accountability, and ethical conduct in the process of making decisions.

The management of risks plays a crucial role in promoting business continuity and resilience by proactively anticipating and making preparations for potential disruptions. The identification of risks that may have adverse effects on the operations, reputation, or financial stability of organizations is facilitated by this process. Risk management enables organizations to devise tactics aimed at mitigating the effects of disruptions, facilitating prompt recovery, and ensuring the uninterrupted continuation of operations.

Risk management enables the acquisition of knowledge and enhancement of performance by documenting insights derived from previous risks and their mitigation. Organizations have the ability to assess and appraise the efficacy of their risk management tactics and modify their methodology in accordance with feedback and experiential knowledge. The iterative process of ongoing learning serves to bolster the risk management competencies of the organization and provides valuable insights for future strategic decision-making.

The incorporation of risk management into strategic decision-making procedures enables organizations to make well-informed choices, proactively identify and mitigate potential risks, and improve their capacity to attain strategic objectives while effectively managing uncertainties. The implementation of risk management strategies offers a methodical and forward-thinking approach to effectively navigate the intricate and unpredictable business landscape, thereby enhancing the probability of achieving favorable strategic results.

9.4 Incorporating Sustainability in Strategic Decision Making

The integration of sustainability into strategic decision-making entails the contemplation of the enduring ecological, societal, and financial ramifications of choices, with the aim of guaranteeing the sustainable and ethical operation of the organization. The process entails the incorporation of sustainability principles and practices into the strategic planning process, evaluation of the sustainability ramifications of strategic alternatives, and the adoption of decisions that are consistent with sustainable development objectives. The following are essential elements that underscore the integration of sustainability in the process of strategic decision making:

The integration of sustainability into an organization's operations commences with the establishment of unambiguous sustainability goals and objectives that are consistent with the organization's vision and values. The objectives may encompass minimizing the ecological footprint, advocating for fair distribution of resources, augmenting stakeholder involvement, or optimizing resource utilization[18]. Establishing unambiguous objectives offers a structure for making informed choices and guarantees the incorporation of sustainability factors into strategic decisions.

Incorporating sustainability into strategic decision-making requires the adoption of a life cycle approach, which involves considering the entire life cycle of a product or process. A comprehensive approach is necessary to account for the complete life cycle of products, services, or initiatives, encompassing the stages of raw material extraction, production, utilization, and disposal. Through a comprehensive assessment of the ecological and societal ramifications throughout the entirety of a product or service's existence, entities can arrive at more knowledgeable determinations that mitigate adverse consequences and optimize favorable results.

In the realm of strategic decision making, it is imperative to evaluate and mitigate the environmental ramifications that may arise from various activities, products, or

---

[18] Eisenhardt, K. M., & Martin, J. A. (2000). Dynamic Capabilities: What Are They? Strategic Management Journal, 21(10-11), 1105-1121.

services. This may entail the assessment of energy consumption, greenhouse gas emissions, waste generation, water utilization, and pollution. The integration of sustainability necessitates the contemplation of ecological aspects in the process of decision-making. This may involve the adoption of sustainable energy sources, the reduction of waste generation, or the implementation of eco-friendly practices.

Incorporating social responsibility into strategic decision-making processes is imperative, as it entails taking into account the social impacts of such decisions. This entails assessing the impact of decisions on various stakeholders, including employees, communities, customers, and other relevant parties. When making decisions, it is imperative for decision makers to take into account various factors including labor practices, human rights, diversity and inclusion, community engagement, and product safety. The integration of social responsibility necessitates making choices that promote the overall welfare of society and facilitate sustainable progress.

Incorporating stakeholder engagement is a crucial aspect of strategic decision-making that warrants significant attention. The insights offered by stakeholders can be of significant value in the context of sustainability issues, as they can aid in the identification of potential risks and opportunities. Incorporating stakeholder engagement throughout the decision-making process facilitates the inclusion of a wide range of perspectives, leading to decisions that are better aligned with societal expectations and needs.

The sustainability of the supply chain should be taken into account when making strategic decisions regarding supply chain management. The process entails the assessment and choice of vendors on the basis of their ecological and societal conduct. Enterprises have the ability to advance sustainable sourcing methodologies, ethical management of supply chains, and conscientious procurement choices. The integration of sustainability practices across the supply chain is crucial in maintaining the organization's sustainability objectives and values.

The integration of sustainability into performance measurement and reporting necessitates the identification of essential KPIs for monitoring progress and the consistent communication of sustainability performance updates. This facilitates the ability of organizations to monitor their sustainability endeavors, disseminate advancements to interested parties, and pinpoint opportunities for enhancement. The implementation of strong measurement and reporting systems promotes responsibility and openness in the process of making strategic decisions.

The strategic decisions pertaining to sustainability challenges should be aimed at exploring opportunities for collaboration and partnerships. Collaborating with industry peers, non-governmental organizations, governmental entities, and other relevant stakeholders has the potential to foster joint efforts that result in favorable transformations. Collaboration enables organizations to harness the combined knowledge, assets, and impact to address intricate sustainability challenges.

The integration of sustainability necessitates the cultivation of a culture that values innovation and adaptation. The promotion and implementation of sustainable practices, technologies, and business models should be fostered and facilitated through strategic decision making. The process entails adopting novel methodologies and persistently pursuing inventive remedies to promote sustainability objectives.

Strategic decision-making ought to prioritize adherence to pertinent environmental, social, and governance (ESG) regulations and standards in order to maintain regulatory compliance and ethical conduct. It is imperative for organizations to uphold ethical business practices, maintain integrity, and conform to relevant legal regulations. The establishment of compliance and ethical conduct serves as a fundamental basis for the attainment of sustainable decision-making.

Through the integration of sustainability into strategic decision-making processes, organizations can effectively align their actions with global sustainability agendas, while simultaneously mitigating negative impacts and generating value for stakeholders.

Chapter 10: Evaluation and Control

In this chapter, we delve deeper into the final steps of the decision-making process. These include evaluating the decision's effectiveness and controlling the course of action based on the evaluation.

10.1 The Importance of Evaluation and Control

The incorporation of evaluation and control mechanisms is crucial in ensuring the efficacy of management and decision-making procedures. Their role is pivotal in ensuring the attainment of organizational goals, efficient utilization of resources, and prompt implementation of corrective measures, if required. The significance of evaluation and control can be underscored by several key reasons.

The process of performance monitoring involves the evaluation and control of organizational performance to determine progress towards achieving strategic goals and objectives. Through consistent assessment of performance metrics, entities can pinpoint both strengths and weaknesses, enabling them to enhance their operations. The act of monitoring performance is crucial in ensuring that actions and decisions are in accordance with the intended outcomes. It also offers valuable insights that aid in making informed decisions.

Evaluation and control mechanisms foster accountability and responsibility among members of an organization. Through the implementation of performance metrics and regular progress tracking, both individuals and teams can be held responsible for their actions and outcomes. The process of evaluation serves as a foundation for providing feedback, recognition, and rewards, which in turn serve as motivators for individuals to assume accountability for their duties and aim for exceptional performance.

Evaluation and control mechanisms assist organizations in identifying any deviations from their predetermined plans or objectives, thereby enabling them to undertake corrective actions and adaptations. In situations where performance fails to meet anticipated standards, the process of evaluation serves to identify specific areas in need of improvement. This, in turn, allows organizations to make necessary adjustments to their strategies, allocate resources more effectively, and implement changes to their processes or practices. The ability to adapt enables organizations to effectively respond to dynamic circumstances and sustain their competitive advantage.

The process of evaluating and controlling resources is crucial for optimizing their utilization. Through consistent monitoring and evaluation of resource allocation, organizations have the ability to pinpoint inefficiencies or instances of wastage. The aforementioned process facilitates well-informed decision-making with respect to resource allocation, thereby guaranteeing that resources are channeled towards endeavors that yield the greatest return on investment and align with strategic objectives.

Evaluation and control mechanisms offer prospects for acquiring knowledge and achieving ongoing enhancement. Through the examination of performance metrics and the assessment of results, institutions can ascertain valuable insights, optimal methodologies, and opportunities for improvement. The implementation of a feedback loop facilitates the ability of organizations to make well-informed modifications, enhance their strategies, and optimize their decision-making procedures in a progressive manner.

Decision-making Evaluation and control mechanisms offer significant insights and information that aid in the decision-making process. Through the monitoring of performance indicators and the analysis of data, decision-makers are able to evaluate the efficacy of past decisions, assess the impact of current strategies, and make more informed choices for the future[19]. The process of evaluation provides a foundation for decision making that is grounded in empirical evidence, thereby mitigating the potential influence of subjective biases.

The attainment of transparency and effective communication with stakeholders is facilitated by the implementation of evaluation and control measures. Organizations exhibit their dedication to accountability and furnish stakeholders with a lucid comprehension of organizational performance by disseminating evaluation outcomes and reporting on performance. The implementation of transparent evaluation procedures has been shown to have a positive impact on various aspects of organizational performance, including the promotion of trust among stakeholders, the facilitation of stakeholder engagement, and the provision of opportunities for constructive feedback.

Risk management involves the assessment and mitigation of potential risks and uncertainties through the implementation of evaluation and control measures. Through consistent performance evaluation and vigilant monitoring of critical indicators, organizations can identify incipient risk signals and adopt preemptive measures to alleviate them. The process of evaluation presents a chance to appraise potential hazards, scrutinize tactics for managing risks, and verify the efficacy of measures taken to mitigate risks.

The assessment and management of compliance and regulatory requirements are crucial for organizations to fulfill their obligations in this regard. Evaluation and control measures are employed to ensure that these requirements are met effectively. Through the assessment of procedures and results, entities can guarantee their compliance with relevant legislation, rules, and professional norms. The process of evaluation serves as a means of ensuring that organizations are conducting their

[19] Norton, D. P., & Kaplan, R. S. (1996). Using the Balanced Scorecard as a Strategic Management System. Harvard Business Review, 74(1), 75-85.

operations in an ethical manner and in compliance with legal mandates, thereby reducing the likelihood of incurring penalties or harm to their reputation.

Evaluation and control mechanisms are instrumental in fostering organizational alignment and coordination. Through the assessment of performance across diverse functions and departments, organizations can discern areas of incongruity, foster cooperation, and guarantee that all facets of the organization are striving towards common objectives. The process of evaluation facilitates the development of a collaborative and collectively accountable environment, thereby augmenting the efficacy of the organization.

In brief, the implementation of evaluation and control mechanisms is imperative for the attainment of efficient management and informed decision-making. These tools aid in the monitoring of performance, ensuring accountability, optimizing resources, promoting learning, managing risks, and facilitating communication with stakeholders. goals, and improve overall performance. The implementation of evaluation and control mechanisms allows organizations to monitor and assess their progress towards achieving predetermined objectives, identify areas for improvement, and make necessary adjustments to their strategies. This approach enables organizations to optimize their resources and ensure that they are allocating them effectively to achieve their desired outcomes. Ultimately, the integration of evaluation and control processes can lead to improved organizational performance and a competitive advantage in the marketplace.

10.2 Evaluation

Evaluation is a methodical approach to evaluating and assessing the efficacy, productivity, and influence of initiatives, schemes, regulations, or undertakings. The process entails the collection and examination of data, juxtaposing factual results with anticipated or preferred results, and formulating evaluations or suggestions based on the discoveries. Assessment holds significant value in serving multiple crucial objectives and providing diverse advantages. The following are essential elements that underscore the significance of evaluation:

The process of evaluation aids in gauging the efficacy of programs or activities in attaining their predetermined goals and objectives. The aforementioned statement offers valuable insights into the attainment of desired results and facilitates the identification of factors that either facilitated or impeded the accomplishment of objectives. The process of assessing the efficacy of programs or activities empowers organizations to make well-informed decisions regarding the continuation, modification, or cessation of said initiatives.

Evaluation is a means of promoting accountability by evaluating the performance and impact of organizations or individuals responsible for implementing programs or projects. The provision of evidence pertaining to progress and outcomes enables stakeholders to hold responsible parties accountable for their actions. The outcomes of evaluations have the potential to provide valuable insights for conducting performance reviews, making informed decisions regarding the allocation of resources, and determining the distribution of rewards and incentives.

Evaluation plays a crucial role in promoting organizational learning and improvement by pinpointing areas of strength, weakness, and opportunities for enhancement. The feedback obtained is of significant value as it sheds light on the strengths and areas for improvement in forthcoming initiatives. The results of evaluations have the potential to guide the establishment of optimal methodologies, the enhancement of tactics, and the implementation of empirically-supported techniques.

The utilization of evaluation in decision-making processes is grounded in evidence-based practices, as it provides empirical data to support the decision-making process. Through the process of assessing the results and effects of various alternatives, individuals in positions of authority can arrive at better-informed decisions. Assessment serves to mitigate dependence on subjective viewpoints and facilitates the formulation of decisions grounded in objective substantiation, thereby enhancing the probability of attaining intended results.

The process of evaluation aids in the optimization of resource allocation through the identification of inefficiencies or wastage in various areas. This aids in assessing the effectiveness and efficiency of resource utilization towards the attainment of desired outcomes. The results of evaluations have the potential to provide valuable insights for decision-making regarding the allocation of resources, budgeting procedures, and cost-effectiveness assessments, ultimately leading to enhanced management of resources.

The process of evaluation is designed to promote stakeholder engagement and participation by actively involving them in the evaluation process. Incorporating stakeholders in the evaluation process serves to guarantee that their viewpoints and input are taken into account, thereby augmenting the credibility and applicability of evaluation outcomes. The active involvement of stakeholders promotes cooperation, responsibility, and answerability in the execution of programs and the process of making decisions.

The act of disseminating evaluation findings to stakeholders fosters transparency and facilitates efficient communication. The act of disclosing evaluation outcomes in a clear and unambiguous manner enhances the level of reliance, authenticity, and answerability. The provision of rationale behind decisions, progress tracking, and impact assessment enables stakeholders to comprehend the situation. The dissemination of evaluation results can promote knowledge transfer and exchange among various organizations or industries.

Evaluation plays a significant role in the enhancement and refinement of policies and programs. The results of evaluations can provide valuable insights for shaping, executing, and adjusting policies by highlighting deficiencies, problematic aspects, or unforeseen outcomes. Evaluation findings can be utilized by policymakers to improve current policies or create new policies that are more closely aligned with intended outcomes and tackle emerging issues.

Continuous monitoring and adaptive management are facilitated by the process of evaluation, which offers valuable feedback on ongoing initiatives. Periodic assessment facilitates prompt modifications, empowering institutions to react to evolving situations or nascent concerns. It fosters a culture of education, flexibility, and ongoing enhancement within entities.

The process of evaluation is instrumental in determining external accountability and funding outcomes. Organizations may be subjected to evaluation as part of their accountability mechanisms by external stakeholders, including donors, funding agencies, or regulatory bodies. The outcomes of evaluations can exert an impact on decisions regarding funding, as they furnish proof of an organization's efficacy and influence the distribution of resources.

Through the process of conducting evaluations, organizations can acquire valuable insights into their performance, which can be utilized to enhance decision-making, accountability, and foster a culture of continuous learning and improvement. The process of evaluation is instrumental in enabling organizations to optimize their effectiveness, guarantee the economical utilization of resources, and provide superior outcomes for their stakeholders.

10.3 Control

Control is the process of observing and policing organizational activities to make sure they are in line with plans, objectives, and established standards. It is used in the management context. The process entails the quantification of performance, juxtaposing it against predetermined objectives, and implementing remedial measures as required. The implementation of control mechanisms serves multiple significant functions and provides diverse advantages. The following are essential elements that underscore the significance of control:

The implementation of control mechanisms enables organizations to gauge and evaluate their performance through performance measurement. Control systems establish a framework for assessing the attainment of goals and objectives through the establishment of performance targets and the monitoring of progress. Performance measurement facilitates the identification of both successful and deficient areas, thereby enabling organizations to undertake suitable measures.

The achievement of goals: Control guarantees that the actions carried out within an organization are in accordance with predetermined plans and objectives. Continuous monitoring of progress and making necessary adjustments facilitates the attainment of desired outcomes. Control systems enable entities to detect variances from predetermined objectives and implement remedial measures to restore alignment, thereby enhancing the probability of achieving desired outcomes.

The process of resource allocation can be optimized through the implementation of control mechanisms that enable the monitoring of resource utilization and the identification of any instances of inefficiency or wastage. The optimization of resource allocation is a crucial factor for organizations to ensure effective and efficient support of their objectives. Control systems offer valuable insights into the utilization of resources and facilitate informed decision-making with respect to resource allocation.

The management of risks is heavily reliant on control measures. Control systems aid in the identification of potential risks and deviations from established norms or standards by monitoring activities and performance. The prompt identification of potential issues enables entities to promptly implement remedial measures and minimize potential hazards. The implementation of control measures plays a vital role in mitigating risks and ensuring their efficient management within acceptable thresholds.

The utilization of control mechanisms can furnish significant data for the purpose of decision making. Organizations can make well-informed decisions by closely monitoring performance indicators that provide real-time data. Control systems facilitate the assessment of various strategies or courses of action, empowering decision-makers to select the most suitable alternative. The implementation of control mechanisms improves the caliber of decision-making processes by guaranteeing that decisions are founded on dependable and precise data.

The implementation of control mechanisms is instrumental in ensuring adherence to legal statutes, regulatory frameworks, and internal policies, thereby promoting compliance and governance. Control systems facilitate the identification and resolution of non-compliance concerns within organizations through the monitoring of activities and performance. The implementation of control mechanisms plays a crucial role in fostering effective governance practices through the facilitation of transparency, accountability, and ethical conduct. The implementation of established standards and guidelines is ensured in organizational activities.

The utilization of control systems facilitates the provision of feedback regarding organizational performance, thereby enabling the acquisition of knowledge through experiential learning. Through the examination of performance data, entities can pinpoint areas that require improvement and formulate tactics to augment forthcoming performance. Control systems enable a culture of ongoing learning, enabling entities to adjust and enhance their procedures, methodologies, and decision-making competencies over a period.

The implementation of control systems has been found to foster both employee motivation and accountability within organizations. Control systems facilitate the establishment of accountability and ownership by defining performance objectives and furnishing evaluations of individual and group performance. Research suggests that employees tend to exhibit higher levels of motivation when they are provided with unambiguous performance expectations and are acknowledged for their accomplishments. Control systems are instrumental in promoting performance-oriented work environments and cultivating a culture of responsibility among staff members.

The concept of organizational alignment posits that control mechanisms are instrumental in ensuring coherence and consistency across various functional units within an organization. Control systems facilitate the identification of areas of misalignment and promote coordination by monitoring activities and performance across various functions or departments. Control systems enable effective communication, cooperation, and dissemination of optimal methodologies, guaranteeing that all sectors of the enterprise strive towards shared aims and objectives.

The implementation of control systems aids in the process of continuous improvement by detecting opportunities for improvement and enabling the establishment of feedback mechanisms. Through the process of performance monitoring, organizations can detect potential areas for process improvement, innovation, or quality enhancement. The implementation of control systems fosters a culture of ongoing enhancement, empowering entities to adjust, create, and maintain competitiveness in a constantly evolving commercial landscape.

In brief, the implementation of control mechanisms is imperative for proficient administration and triumph of an organization. This statement highlights the various benefits of utilizing performance measurement techniques in organizational management. These benefits include the ability to evaluate performance, attain objectives, optimize resource allocation, manage risks, facilitate decision-making processes, ensure compliance, promote learning, motivate employees, align activities, and drive continuous improvement. Control systems equip organizations with the necessary resources and knowledge to oversee, manage, and enhance their performance, thereby augmenting their capacity to attain desired objectives.

10.4 Tools for Evaluation and Control

There are numerous tools and techniques for evaluation and control that can be used to keep track of organizational performance, gauge how far we've come toward our goals, and pinpoint areas where we need to get better. The following are frequently utilized instruments for assessment and regulation:

Key Performance Indicators (KPIs) are metrics, either quantitative or qualitative, that are utilized to assess performance and advancement towards strategic objectives. Key Performance Indicators (KPIs) offer a systematic approach to monitoring and evaluating particular metrics, enabling the comparison of such metrics against predetermined targets or benchmarks. Key Performance Indicators (KPIs) encompass a variety of metrics that organizations use to evaluate their performance. These metrics may include revenue growth, customer satisfaction ratings, employee productivity, and quality metrics. Key Performance Indicators (KPIs) facilitate the monitoring of performance and the identification of areas that necessitate attention or enhancement.

The Balanced Scorecard is a comprehensive framework that offers a multifaceted perspective of organizational performance by taking into account various dimensions. The framework encompasses various perspectives, namely financial, customer, internal processes, and learning and growth. The Balanced Scorecard methodology facilitates the synchronization of performance metrics with strategic goals and delivers an equitable evaluation of organizational performance across multiple domains.

Dashboards refer to graphical displays that present essential performance metrics and data. These tools offer a succinct and expedient summary of performance, allowing individuals to track progress in real-time. Customizable dashboards facilitate the display of pertinent information, enabling decision-makers to discern patterns, anomalies, and problematic areas. Dashboards are a valuable tool for monitoring performance in relation to predetermined objectives and promoting decision-making based on data analysis.

Benchmarking is a process that entails evaluating the performance and practices of an organization in comparison to industry standards or best practices. This practice facilitates the identification of both proficient and deficient domains. The practice of benchmarking can be conducted through internal means, whereby performance is compared across various departments or divisions within the organization, or through external means, whereby performance is compared against industry standards or competitors. Benchmarking is a valuable tool that can offer valuable insights into areas where an organization may be underperforming or exceeding expectations.

Performance appraisals refer to the evaluation of individual employee performance based on predetermined goals and objectives. The provision of feedback on performance, identification of areas for improvement, and support for employee development are among the key functions of these individuals. Performance evaluations may be carried out via structured assessments, self-evaluations, or evaluations by colleagues. Performance management systems aid in the synchronization of individual performance with the objectives of the organization and the enhancement of overall performance.

Quality control tools are utilized to oversee and regulate the quality of products or processes. These tools include Pareto charts, cause-and-effect diagrams, control charts, and process capability analysis. The aforementioned tools facilitate the identification of underlying causes of quality-related concerns, monitoring of fluctuations, and implementation of remedial measures to enhance quality performance.

Financial analysis tools, including financial ratios, trend analysis, and variance analysis, are utilized to assess financial performance and manage financial resources. The aforementioned tools facilitate the evaluation of an organization's profitability, liquidity, solvency, and efficiency. Financial analysis tools offer valuable insights into the financial strengths and weaknesses of an organization, thereby empowering decision-makers to make informed financial decisions.

Internal audit pertains to impartial and detached evaluations of organizational procedures, safeguards, and adherence to policies and regulations. The function of internal auditors is to assess the adequacy of internal controls, identify potential risks, and provide recommendations for enhancing efficiency and effectiveness. The function of internal audit is to furnish management and stakeholders with the assurance that appropriate controls are established and that operational risks are being effectively managed.

The utilization of customer feedback and surveys is a valuable approach to assess customer satisfaction, loyalty, and perceptions of an organization's products or services. The aforementioned insights offer valuable information regarding the requirements, inclinations, and potential enhancements in the customer experience. The utilization of customer feedback and surveys can aid in the identification of opportunities to improve customer experience and address any deficiencies in service delivery.

Project management tools, including Gantt charts, project schedules, and progress reports, are employed to oversee and regulate project performance. The aforementioned tools facilitate the monitoring of project milestones, detection of possible hindrances or constraints, and assurance of adherence to predetermined schedules and financial plans. Project management tools facilitate project monitoring and allow project managers to implement corrective measures as needed.

When utilized effectively, these instruments empower entities to assess and manage their productivity, pinpoint opportunities for enhancement, and arrive at informed determinations that elevate comprehensive efficiency and accomplish strategic goals. The choice of particular instruments is contingent upon the type of institution, the goals under scrutiny, and the information accessible for examination.

10.5 Challenges in Evaluation and Control

Although evaluation and control are crucial for managing organizational performance, they can pose several challenges that organizations must confront. Several typical obstacles encountered in the process of evaluation and control are as follows:

The acquisition of precise and dependable data for assessment purposes can present difficulties in terms of both availability and quality. Data collection can pose a challenge for organizations, particularly in the absence of requisite systems and processes. Insufficient or erroneous data may result in erroneous assessments and suboptimal decision-making. The maintenance of data availability, accuracy, and consistency necessitates the implementation of appropriate data management systems and the establishment of resilient data collection procedures.

Selecting suitable metrics and performance indicators is a critical aspect of achieving effective evaluation and control. The process of identifying metrics that accurately align with an organization's goals and objectives can present a formidable task. It is imperative for organizations to meticulously deliberate upon the pertinence, quantifiability, and congruity of metrics in relation to their strategic priorities. Inadequate or imprecise metrics may result in misapprehension and suboptimal assessment of performance.

The evaluation processes may be susceptible to the influence of subjectivity and bias. The objectivity and fairness of evaluations may be impacted by evaluators' personal biases or varying interpretations. Establishing unambiguous evaluation criteria, imparting adequate training to evaluators, and incorporating measures to alleviate biases and guarantee uniformity in evaluations are crucial.

The process of evaluation and control necessitates the allocation of time, resources, and focused endeavors. Organizations may encounter restrictions with respect to the resources at their disposal, financial limitations, and conflicting priorities. The scarcity of resources can have an adverse effect on the thoroughness and regularity of assessments, thereby posing difficulties in achieving a holistic comprehension of performance and executing efficacious regulatory strategies.

Organizations frequently function within intricate settings that entail numerous interrelated elements that impact their operational efficacy[20]. Assessing and managing performance within intricate systems can present difficulties. Attributing outcomes solely to specific decisions or initiatives can be challenging due to the difficulty in isolating the impact of particular actions or variables on performance.

Organizational change initiatives may encounter opposition from personnel or interested parties who may experience unease with the prospect of being evaluated or monitored during the process of evaluation and control. The reluctance to undergo evaluation can have detrimental effects on the efficiency of control mechanisms and impede endeavors aimed at enhancing organizational performance. The cultivation of a culture that prioritizes the advantages of evaluation and control, accentuates learning and growth, and tackles apprehensions and oppositions through proficient communication and involvement is crucial.

Achieving a balance between short-term performance and long-term sustainability is crucial in the process of evaluation and control. Organizations may encounter pressure to prioritize immediate outcomes over enduring goals. Placing excessive emphasis on immediate objectives may result in shortsighted decision-making and disregard for crucial elements that are instrumental in achieving enduring prosperity, such as sustainability, employee growth, and innovation.

It is imperative that the evaluation and control processes are aligned with the culture and values of the organization. In the event that assessment procedures are viewed as retributive, they have the potential to engender an atmosphere of apprehension and impede openness and cooperation. The cultivation of a culture that prioritizes learning, enhancement, and responsibility, alongside the appreciation of transparent communication and productive criticism, is of utmost significance.

---

[20] Simons, R. (1995). Levers of Control: How Managers Use Innovative Control Systems to Drive Strategic Renewal. Harvard Business Press.

To tackle these obstacles, it is necessary to adopt a proactive stance, employ efficient communication methods, secure organizational dedication, and strive for ongoing enhancement. It is recommended that organizations allocate resources towards the implementation of comprehensive data management systems, define unambiguous standards for evaluation, offer guidance and assistance to evaluators, and cultivate a work environment that places a high degree of importance on evaluation and regulation as means of enhancing knowledge and progress. Through the resolution of these obstacles, entities can optimize the efficiency of their assessment and regulation procedures, ultimately leading to improved performance results.

Bibliography

1. Andersson, S. (2011). International entrepreneurship, born globals and the theory of effectuation. Journal of Small Business and Enterprise Development, 18(3), 627–643.
2. Apergis, N., Fafaliou, I., & Polemis, M. L. (2016). New evidence on assessing the level of competition in the European Union banking sector: A panel data approach. International Business Review, 25(1), 395–407.
3. Ariely, D. (2008). Predictably Irrational: The Hidden Forces That Shape Our Decisions. HarperCollins.
4. Baack, D., Wilson, R. T., van Dessel, M. M., & Patti, C. H. (2015). Advertising to business: Does creativity matter? Industrial Marketing Management available online 30 October 2015 10.1016/j.indmarman.2015.10.001
5. Baron, R. A. (2006). Opportunity recognition as pattern recognition: How entrepreneurs "connect the dots" to identify new business opportunities. Academy of Management Perspectives, 20(1), 104–119.
6. Bauer, J. C., Schmitt, P., Morwitz, V. G., & Winer, R. S. (2013). Managerial decision making in customer management: Adaptive, fast and frugal? Journal of the Academy of Marketing Science, 41(4), 436–455.
7. Bjerke, B., & Hultman, C. M. (2002). Entrepreneurial marketing – The growth of small firms in the new economic era. Cheltenham, U.K.: Edward Elgar Publishing.
8. Blatter, J. K. (2008). Case study. In L. M. Given (Ed.), The SAGE encyclopaedia of qualitative research methods (pp. 68–71).
9. Brown, S., & Eisenhardt, K. M. (1997). The art of continuous change: Linking complexity theory and time-paced evolution in relentlessly shifting organizations. Administrative Science Quarterly, 42(1), 1–34.

10. Carson, D., & Coviello, N. (1996). Qualitative research issues at the marketing/entrepreneurship interface. Marketing Intelligence & Planning, 14(6), 51–58.
11. Carson, D., Cromie, S., McGowan, P., & Hill, J. (1995). Marketing and entrepreneurship in SMEs – An innovative approach. London: Prentice Hall.
12. Castle, E. N., Becker, M. H., & Smith, F. J. (1972). Farm business management: the decision making process. *Farm business management: the decision making process. Second Edition.*
13. Chandy, R. K., & Tellis, G. J. (2000). The incumbent's curse? Incumbency, size, and radical product innovation. Journal of Marketing, 64(3), 1–17.
14. Davenport, T. H., & Harris, J. G. (2007). Competing on Analytics: The New Science of Winning. Harvard Business School Press.
15. Drucker, P. F. (1990). The Role of Decision Making in Management. Harvard Business Review, 68(3), 111-120.
16. Eisenhardt, K. M., & Martin, J. A. (2000). Dynamic Capabilities: What Are They? Strategic Management Journal, 21(10-11), 1105-1121.
17. Grant, R. M. (2003). Strategic Planning in a Turbulent Environment: Evidence from the Oil Majors. Strategic Management Journal, 24(6), 491-517.
18. Hughes, P., & Morgan, R. E. (2007). A resource-advantage perspective of product–market strategy performance & strategic capital in high technology firms. Industrial Marketing Management, 36(4), 503–517.
19. Järvensivu, T., & Törnroos, J.-Å. (2010). Case study research with moderate constructionism: Conceptualization and practical illustration. Industrial Marketing Management, 39, 100–108.
20. Jaworski, B., Kohli, A. K., & Sahay, A. (2000). Market-driven versus driving markets. Journal of the Academy of Marketing Science, 28(1), 45–54
21. Keeney, R. L., & Raiffa, H. (1976). Decisions with Multiple Objectives: Preferences and Value Tradeoffs. Wiley.

22.Khan, S. A., & Zafar, M. W. (2013). Multi-Criteria Decision Making: A Comparative Study. International Journal of Operations Research and Information Systems, 4(4), 15-29.

23.Klein, G. (2008). Naturalistic Decision Making. Human Factors, 50(3), 456-460.

24.Malhotra, N. K., & Birks, D. F. (2007). Marketing Research: An Applied Approach. Pearson Education.

25.March, J. G. (1994). A Primer on Decision Making: How Decisions Happen. The Free Press.

26.Mintzberg, H., Raisinghani, D., & Theoret, A. (1976). The Structure of Unstructured Decision Processes. Administrative Science Quarterly, 21(2), 246-275.

27.Morris, M. H., Schindehutte, M., & LaForge, R. W. (2002). Entrepreneurial marketing: A construct for integrating emerging entrepreneurship and marketing perspectives. Journal of Marketing Theory and Practice, 10(4), 1–19.

28.Mort, G. S., Weerawardena, J., & Liesch, P. (2012). Advancing entrepreneurial marketing: Evidence from born global firms. European Journal of Marketing, 46(3), 542–562.

29.Mowen, J. C., & Gaeth, G. J. (1992). The evaluation stage in marketing decision making. Journal of the Academy of Marketing Science, 20(2), 177–187.

30.Murray, J. A. (1981). Marketing is home for the entrepreneurial process. Industrial Marketing Management, 10, 93–99.

31.Nijssen, E. J. (2014). Entrepreneurial marketing: An effectual approach. New York: Routledge.

32.Norton, D. P., & Kaplan, R. S. (1996). Using the Balanced Scorecard as a Strategic Management System. Harvard Business Review, 74(1), 75-85.

33.Osborn, A. F. (1953). Applied Imagination: Principles and Procedures of Creative Problem Solving. Charles Scribner's Sons.

34.Robinson, J. (2020). The Importance of Decision Making in Business. Journal of Business Administration, 45(2), 12-25.

35.Simon, H. A. (1960). The New Science of Management Decision. Prentice Hall.

36.Simons, R. (1995). Levers of Control: How Managers Use Innovative Control Systems to Drive Strategic Renewal. Harvard Business Press.

37.Sharma, R., Mithas, S., & Kankanhalli, A. (2014). Transforming decision-making processes: a research agenda for understanding the impact of business analytics on organisations. *European Journal of Information Systems*, *23*(4), 433-441.

38.Thousand Oaks, CA: Sage Publications, Inc. Blocker, C. P., Flint, D. J., Myers, M. B., & Slater, S. F. (2011). Proactive customer orientation and its role for creating customer value in global markets. Journal of the Academy of Marketing Science, 39(2), 216–233.

39.Tjosvold, D., & Johnson, D. W. (2017). Conflict and Cooperation: Intragroup and Intergroup Perspectives. Routledge.

40.Treviño, L. K., & Nelson, K. A. (2016). Managing Business Ethics: Straight Talk about How to Do It Right. Wiley.

41.Tversky, A., & Kahneman, D. (1974). Judgment under Uncertainty: Heuristics and Biases. Science, 185(4157), 1124-1131.

42.Velasquez, M. (2012). Business Ethics: Concepts and Cases. Pearson.

43.Yin, R. K. (2009). Case study research: Design and methods. London: Sage Publications.

44.Zahra, S. A. (2005). A theory of international new ventures: A decade of research. Journal of International Business Studies, 36(1), 20–28.

www.ingramcontent.com/pod-product-compliance
Lightning Source LLC
LaVergne TN
LVHW022100200926
848481LV00003B/1009